HD
58.7
.L68
2004

Work Culture Transformation
Straw to Gold - The Modern Hero's Journey

Evie Lotze

Work Culture Transformation

Straw to Gold – The Modern Hero's Journey

K · G · Saur München 2004

Bibliographic information published by Die Deutsche Bibliothek
Die Deutsche Bibliothek lists this publication in the Deutsche Nationalbibliografie;
detailed bibliographic data is available in the internet at http://dnb.ddb.de.

∞
Printed on acid-free paper
© 2004 K. G. Saur Verlag GmbH, München
All Rights Strictly Reserved
No part of this publication may be reproduced, stored in a retrieval system,
or transmitted in any form or by any means, electronic, mechanical, photocopying,
recording, or otherwise, without permission in writing from the publisher

Typesetting by Florence Production Ltd., Stoodleigh, Devon, Great Britain.

Printed and bound by Strauss GmbH, Mörlenbach, Germany.

ISBN 3-598-11637-3

Dedicated to

Chris Lotze

Co-adventurer par excellence, Anchor, Sword-bearer, Poet, Chief of Support, and staunch Critic when invited – what writer could ask for more?

Contents

Acknowledgments — ix
The Structure of This Book — 1
Once Upon A Time — 3

Section I: Culture, Work and the Knowledge Age — 7
    Chapter 1: Work Culture of the Knowledge Age — 9

Section II: The Modern Hero — 25
    Chapter 2: Heroes — 29
    Chapter 3: The Hero's Transformation — 35

Section III: Universal Stages of Transformation — 45
    Chapter 4: Transformation — 47
    Chapter 5: Four Stages of Transformation — 53
    Chapter 6: Personal and Organizational Transformation — 63

Section IV: From Straw to Gold — 69
    Chapter 7: The Tale of Rumpelstiltskin — 73
    Chapter 8: Why Rumpelstiltskin? — 77
    Chapter 9: Understanding the Tale — 81

Section V: Getting on with the Transformation — 107
    Chapter 10: Equipping for the Journey — 109
    Chapter 11: What Do We Do on Monday Morning? — 119
    Chapter 12: Transforming a Business Psychodramatically — 125

Epilogue: Happily Ever After – give me a break — 137

Appendices — 139
    Appendix I: In-a-nutshell Cheat Sheet on Myths and Fairy Tales — 141
    Appendix II: A Platform for Leaping Into the New Language — 153
    Appendix III: Why We Don't Share Information — 161
    Appendix IV: An Integrated Digital Environment — 169

Appendix V: A Work Culture Transformation Assessment 173
Appendix VI: A Workbook for Transformation 183

Index 187

Acknowledgments

For the crucible of ideas that bubbled up to become this book, I am indebted to the stimulating conversations about the transformation of work from industrial to knowledge work over many long lunches with my colleagues Ken Megill, Ph.D., Noel Dickover, and Herb Schantz. Each of us brought a different perspective to the work we did. Ken Megill, philosopher and author of several books,[1] brought a long history of thinking and writing about change of different kinds. Herb Schantz, an early pioneer of the technologies underlying Optical Character Recognition (OCR) and founder of The Association for Work Process Improvement (TAWPI), brought his formidable knowledge and experience to bear on our thinking about work culture transformation. Noel Dickover, an anthropologist and cyberneticist, kept us honest in our thinking about cultures and about technology as we sought the key to work culture transformation.

I am particularly grateful to the many people who have given the manuscript thoughtful attention and strengthened it in many different ways. Sue Barnum, a dear friend and professional colleague from my incarnation as psychodrama trainer, offered her astute assessment of one of the earliest versions and the psychodrama chapter. Marilyn Barth, Susan Brown, Clare Imholtz, and Deborah Marshall are new colleagues from this present phase; they come from Ken Megill's world and supported our separating what was to have been one book into two. They continue to offer critical and supportive advice to both of us. Noel Dickover has kept me on the straight and narrow not only about technology but also about the business world and, even through his own tumultuous transformation, continued to

---

[1] Megill, Kenneth: Document Management: New Technologies for the Information Services Manager. London: Bowker Saur, 1999. (With Herbert F. Schantz).
Corporate Memory: Information Management in the Electronic Age. London: Bowker Saur, 1997.
Making the Information Revolution. A Handbook on Federal Information Resources Management. Silver Spring, Maryland: Association for Information and Image Management (AIIM), 1995. (With Rose Cummins, Thomas Horan, Sarah Kadec, Marilyn McLennan, Michael McReynolds, Robert Woods.)
The New Democratic Theory. New York: Free Press (Macmillan), 1970.
Thinking for a Living. Munich: Saur, 2004.

make his intelligent observations available. Jolanta Juszkiewicz, friend and colleague from the criminal justice world, brought her keen eye for detail and her sharp wit to bear on the hardly believable world of fairy tale – and read both an early and late version, improving both immeasurably. Katharine Koch, an ally through many adventures, read as the mythical "general intelligent audience" and sharpened many aspects. Chris Lotze, fellow traveler and unerring provider of *hupago* has been cheerleader throughout the long and lonely process. Conrad Lotze, with his father's critical eye for detail and his mother's love of a good story, offered wonderfully keen insight and polish. Kristina Maciunas brought a doctor's sensibility, a gardener's eye for aesthetics, and a gentle way of suggesting change when she read the manuscript. Vincas Maciunas gave willingly of his time and his expertise in the arena of technology and his knowledge of Greece at the time of myths. To Deanna Marcum I am grateful, as always, for her unfailing encouragement and support. Ken Megill got me into this mess and has done penance by standing faithfully by as support, encouragement, and honest critic, casting his intrepid sensate eye on and wrapping his left brain around the project. He also read indefatigably, for which I am eternally grateful. Tim Salony, an old camping buddy from days in the Saudi dessert with a lively interest in dreams, tales, and myths, read the manuscript from his librarian's perspective as one helping transform a library's work culture.

Gerrie Turpie has been a lively, interested, and wonderfully encouraging editor – gracious in her hospitality, kind in her critique, and fun to be with and to work with. To John (Max) MacNamee for his sharp eye for detail and quick wit, I owe thanks for the final thorough copy-editing.

After involvement with the Work Culture Transformation Board of the United States Air Force, my own thinking as a psychotherapist was refocused on the nascent revolution waiting in the wings of the workplace. Those who were trying to midwife this transformation agreed that an outmoded work culture inhibits its birth. I am grateful to Col. Terry Balven, USAF, for the opportunity to work with the Board and for the thinking, encouragement, and critique of each of the many bright and creative colleagues working on that difficult challenge: how to achieve a transformation of the fundamentals of work.

The Structure of This Book

In which we explain the background and ideas that led to the creation of this book.

The structure of this book is dictated by the purpose of this book: to translate what I know of personal transformation into the world of work and to tell the stories of transformation in the language of myths and fairy tales. This language more clearly than any other describes the steps along the road – the journey – to transformation. But today's audiences are often neither familiar with that language nor do they immediately see the relevance of myths and tales to modern life.

Before going into the language of transformation, though, we need to get a glimpse of where the language will prepare us to travel. Therefore, Section I addresses the concept of culture, culture change, and the transformation of the work culture that will usher in the Knowledge Age.

A major part of this book, Section II, presents the background of the modern analysis of myths and tales. This background includes brief sketches of three influential scholars in that area: Joseph Moreno, Carl Jung, and Joseph Campbell. Moreno and Jung were psychiatrists whose work deeply oriented my own practice of psychotherapy that helped clients achieve personal transformations. Joseph Campbell was a cultural anthropologist whose research revealed the universality of the lessons of myths and tales. Understanding the contributions of these intellectuals greatly contributes to understanding the lessons offered by myth and tales.

Section III provides an in-depth examination of transformation. We analyze the stages of the process of transformation by using the metaphor of the hero's journey, the same metaphor used by myth and tale to talk about the human journey through the stages of life.

In Section IV the reader is reacquainted with the fairy tale of Rumpelstiltskin, from which the title of this book is taken, and led through a modern analysis of the tale. Rumpelstiltskin is a tale particularly suited to talking about transformation of a work culture. In this tale the hero is faced with an impossible, insurmountable task: to spin a mountain of straw into gold. The process by which the hero accomplishes this task has much to offer the modern hero who would lead or participate in a work culture transformation. The tale, written in medieval Europe, seems to speak directly to people who experience work as straw but want to make gold. Its voice can be heard equally clearly by those who work with the straw and those who lead the transformation efforts of organizations – the visionaries who know that the "spinning wheel" *can* perform differently: it need make neither thread, nor spew forth untransformed straw. It can, in the right hands, make gold. The same stages (some would say methodology) of transformation apply to both – those stages are part of the knowledge I bring from my experience with individuals and groups caught in the grips of the profound changes that are transformative.

Section V invites the reader to see the process of transformation with the third eye, that eye that sees what our other two more literal eyes cannot. It speaks of what modern heroes need in order to equip themselves for the journey of transformation. It also addresses what the hero willing to embark on the journey does on Monday morning; and telescopes the often long and arduous process into a psychodramatic look at an organization caught in the throes of the imperative to transform.

The Epilogue addresses the modern skepticism of the "happily ever after" endings of fairy tales. The appendices provide thumbnail sketches of the fairy tales to which the author alludes in the book. They also provide a glossary of terms, and an essay on why it is so difficult for us to share information. In the appendices there is also a measurement instrument of work culture transformation, and a workbook to guide the thinking of change agents undertaking leadership of an organizational transformation.

This book addresses the initiation of the modern transformation that will bring us into the Age of Knowledge. It is beyond the scope of this work to address the consequences of that transformation: Who will be left behind? What jobs will be redefined? How will the world adjust to the profound changes? And a myriad of other questions that a new Age will raise. Those are all subjects for future exploration.

Once Upon A Time

Once upon a time in an age long ago there were some people who tried to figure out what made human beings tick. They realized that people did some pretty bizarre things – even those people who functioned well in every day life, even people who were highly successful, never mind those that society had a hard time incorporating. They tried to discover what made human beings alike and what made them different from each other. When enough people started to think about these things, they decided to give the name psychology to their study of human behavior.

Some psychologists went back into history to see how other cultures had sought to answer these same questions. Some of them studied astrology as one of the first attempts to understand influences on human behavior. Others studied alchemy; some turned to the study of the abnormal to ferret out the clues to "normal," while yet others looked at the animal kingdom for parallels. Some turned to the study of stories that had survived from ancient times – myths and fairy tales – for they believed these stories to be "nothing less than the distilled truth about what we call 'real life'."[2]

Those scholars who studied the myths and tales of other cultures discovered basic similarities across cultures, similarities of themes and types of characters. They realized that the myths and tales of ancient cultures were ways to explain how human beings behaved. They found

---

[2] Davies, Robertson. "The Conscience of the Writer." In *One Half of Robertson Davies*. New York: Viking, 1977, p. 131.

that tales were ways to instruct ordinary human beings by using stories about heroes. They taught ways to make life work – the life of individuals and the life of society. These stories themselves were the earliest psychology. They explained how one navigates the territory from birth to death, how members of the society meet the challenges encountered in transforming from immaturity to maturity. These myths and tales of ancient times embody wisdom and insights that are instructive and applicable today, if we can view them symbolically rather than literally.

Transformation

When Christopher Columbus[3] set out on his famous journey of discovery, he had a map of the world – but it was wrong. When he returned from his trip across the part of the map marked "hic sunt animales" ("here are monsters") the knowledge he brought back transformed the ways we thought about the world in which we lived. The world was launched into a new Age of Discovery based on new information, new assumptions – a culture transformation. If the belief in a flat world was shattered by the finding that it was round, what else might Columbus' world need to question?

In the Information Age, we believed that technology would revolutionize our work world. We thought it would so radically change the way our world operated that it would amount to a cultural revolution. Today's technology has changed the way we do many tasks, yet it has not fundamentally changed the way we do our work, the assumptions we bring to that work, the unconscious beliefs we hold about that work. What parts of our current knowledge might we need to question in order to give birth to a new work age, the Age of Knowledge?

A non-historian's overly quick overview of Ages

Once upon a time humans were hunters and gatherers roaming the earth in glorious or uprooted freedom, depending on your point of view. This Age lasted for hundreds of thousands of years. Then, some hunters and gatherers began to settle in permanent locations, saved seeds, planted

---

[3] Columbus did not single-handedly launch the Age of Discovery. He was but one of many involved in dispelling the popular "knowledge" of the world's flatness; educated people had already replaced the old belief. He serves throughout as a convenient symbol – one of many possible heroes of the era.

crops, protected, nurtured, and harvested them. This, in retrospect, was called the Agrarian Age. The first hunters and gatherers who settled into agriculture didn't realize that they were transforming the way work was done – that each new tool would pave the way for ever more accelerated change. The astute reader will notice that we are glossing over the Stone Age and the Bronze Age and others, equally transformative of the way work was done.

As great minds pondered ways to make work ever easier, faster, and more productive, the Industrial Age was born. The craftsman, farmer, and peasant traded the autonomous and risky agrarian life for the safety of the regular job in industry, preferring eating to starving. Machines made the Industrial Age possible. The process of breaking work into smaller and smaller pieces that could be done by workers with less and less training, making the labor cheaper and easier to replace, ushered in the Manufacturing Age. As tools changed once again, the Information Age roared onto the stage.

It can be said that both the Manufacturing and Information Ages are subsets of the culture of the Industrial Age because of the way work is done. Work is still performed in hierarchical organizations. Workers know less and less about the whole, are allowed to hoard information, complete one piece of work and pass it up, assembly-line-fashion, to higher levels for the addition of another layer toward final completion at the top – all hallmarks of the work culture of the Industrial Age.

Now, if we can manage to transform the work culture to support it, the Knowledge Age waits in the wings of history, ready to usher in a new way to do work. This new Age requires a culture exactly the opposite of the Manufacturing Age (breaking work into smaller and smaller pieces) and exactly the opposite of the Industrial Age (machinery dictating the place, the pace, and the pattern of work).

The culture of the Knowledge Age, with its increasingly rapid rate of change, the complexity and interconnectedness of its issues and its communities, will depend on attitudes of collaboration and trust. It will depend on habits of preserving the essential elements of the knowledge created and workers' knowing the larger picture – where their piece of work fits into the whole.

Will we rise to the demands of the journey to this new age?

SECTION I

Culture, Work and the Knowledge Age

In which we discuss culture and work culture and reveal where the journey of work culture transformation can lead us: to the Knowledge Age.

CHAPTER 1

Work Culture of the Knowledge Age

Culture

To talk about cultural transformation, we will begin with a definition of culture. While other definitions are relegated to the platform for leaping into a new language section (Appendix II) this one is so central to this section that it needs immediate discussion.

In looking to anthropology for a definition of culture, we find that there are as many definitions of culture as there are anthropologists. However, one is still alluded to as the classic:

> *That complex whole which includes knowledge, belief, art, morals, law, custom, and any other capabilities and habits acquired by man as a member of society.*[4]

More recently the Modern Dictionary of Sociology[5] generalizes further:

> *The way of life of a social group; the groups' total man-made environment including all the material and nonmaterial products of group life that are transmitted from one generation to the next.*

---

[4] Tylor, E. B. Primitive Culture, V.1. London: John Murray. 1871, p.1.
[5] Theodorson, George & Achilles. A Modern Dictionary of Sociology. NY: Thomas Crowell. 1969.

Other sociologists and anthropologists speak of culture as the whole set of activities through which a human group encompasses and transforms nature, including human nature. In other words, culture is what distinguishes humans from the animal kingdom because it includes all that is produced and transformed by human collectives: language, art, beliefs, attitudes, norms, social structure, and values.

One of the best allusions to the effect of culture on our lives is a recent and very timely manuscript produced for the United Nations:

> *Culture and values are the soul of development. They provide its impetus, facilitate the means needed to further it, and substantially define people's vision of its purposes and ends. Culture and values are instrumental in the sense that they help to shape people's daily hopes, fears, ambitions, attitudes and actions, but they are also formative because they mould people's ideals and inspire their dreams for a fulfilling life for themselves and future generations. There is some debate in Arab countries about whether culture and values promote or retard development. Ultimately, however, values are not the servants of development; they are its wellspring.*[6]

In other words, culture is the whole of the human-made and human-chosen environment in which we live and work; it is both explicit and implicit – one we understand and can articulate and one in which we are not aware of the underlying assumptions of our behavior and thoughts. Culture shades our character, personality, and actions; it informs where we believe ourselves to be in a society. Over the ages it shapes the values we live by as if they were just common sense; it incorporates our belief structure and shapes the very fabric of our being.

In this book we will focus much of our attention on a subset of culture: the culture of work.

Work Culture

As we address work culture in this section, we mean two things. The first we might refer to as culture with a small "c." By this we mean the environment in which work happens. The set of assumptions, under-

---

[6] The *Arab Human Development Report, 2002* written for the United Nations Development Program by a distinguished group of Arab intellectuals can be found in its entirety at http://www.undp.org/rbas/ahdr.

standings, and beliefs shared by a working community that manifests itself with clear and distinct patterns of interaction in a particular workplace. Business literature, particularly the literature of change management, often implies that each workplace has a different culture. The various elements of the particular environment can be changed, even managed and mapped and planned. Significant improvements can be realized. But this view of culture is not profound enough. Culture is much more than the clothes we wear or attitudes we adopt at any particular time or in any particular place. Culture is what we assume, more than what we decide.

The second thing we mean by work culture is the common sense that a worker brings to work.[7] The work culture consists of the shared attitudes toward work, the shared beliefs not about this workplace, but work in general, the common expectations about behavior, the "rituals" of work, the traditions of work, the "way things have always been done." When workers leave one workplace and go to another, there may be minor changes in such things as dress, hours, wires and computers, and mores of talk around the water fountain. But the overall rules that govern such things as whether information is shared and with whom and how, the beliefs about collaboration vs. individual responsibility, or the attitudes about where and when and for how long work is done – these do not change. These are part of what we might well refer to as Work Culture (with capital letters) many elements of which are unconscious, assumed, not examined daily – if at all. They are just the way things are.

In the industrial world, of which we are still a part, that work culture is determined and driven by the machine, the mode of production. The owner/manager of the machines orchestrates the work, whether those machines are robots on the floor of the manufacturing plant or computers in cubicles. We can see this translated into the world of the Information Age where the computer and its capacities and configurations can dominate much of the way work is done today.

In the Age of Knowledge, which we are approaching, the work culture will be driven by the need to access information in order to create knowledge. The wires and computers will enable this information access, not dictate how it is gained, when and where it is shared, or how and where it is stored for reuse.

In the Knowledge Age, work is focused on the creation of knowledge. Information is the raw material of knowledge; knowledge workers take information, process it through their own backgrounds, skills, experience

---

[7] A definition formulated first, I believe, by Ken Megill in his work with the Work Culture Transformation Board.

and judgment and make a decision in the nature of "is it a good idea to . . . ?" This judgment and the essential evidence leading to it are the knowledge created. That knowledge (the judgment and how it was reached) is added to the community's body of knowledge and becomes part of the information others use in creating their knowledge.

> *How we do our work is mostly a matter of habit. These habits are developed, over a period of time in response to the needs of the work place and the tools (technologies) that are available to get the work done.*
>
> *The development of knowledge work as the primary kind of work means we will need new habits to get the work done efficiently and well. Developing these habits requires a transformation of the work culture, for the work culture is made up of the beliefs and expectations that we bring to our work.*[8]

We could translate into the world of business the excellent summation of the importance and all-pervasive nature of culture explicated in the United Nations document by thinking of development in its broader sense. The dictionary definition of *development* is "to bring out the capabilities or possibilities of; to bring to a more advanced or effective state."[9] With this broad definition in mind, let us re-state the effect of culture on our work lives.

> *The culture, in which we live or work, drives the advancement of our personal, professional, and business lives. The culture provides the impetus for bringing out the capabilities and possibilities of life; it facilitates the means needed to further those capabilities and possibilities; and culture substantially defines people's vision of personal, professional and business purposes and ends; it directs the patterns of interaction among people. Culture and values are instrumental in that they help to shape people's daily hopes, fears, ambitions, attitudes and actions. Culture is also formative because it molds people's ideals and inspires their dreams for a fulfilling life for themselves and future generations. There is some debate in the business world about whether the present work culture and values promote or retard development. Ultimately, however, the values of our culture are the source from which the most effective state of our personal, professional and business lives spring.*

---

[8] Megill, Kenneth. Thinking for a Living. Munich: Saur, 2004, p. 51
[9] Random House College Dictionary.

Work Culture of the Knowledge Age 13

To change something so basic to our lives that it informs every aspect – our vision, our patterns of interaction, our hopes, fears, ambitions, attitudes, actions, dreams – is a formidable task, a task of heroic proportions.

To make a transformation from today's industrial culture to a culture that would make real knowledge work possible will be a bit like creating a garden on the site of a nuclear dump.[10] First the artifacts of the nuclear dump have to be cleared. Then the soil has to be decontaminated. Next, new fertile soil has to be imported and mixed into the ground of the old dump. Finally, any remaining weeds from the old site will have to be pulled before the seeds of the new garden can grow.

If we are to transform the work culture born of the Industrial Revolution (and in support of its specific needs) to one that supports the needs of the Age of Knowledge, we return to the United Nations Report and begin with an appreciation of what a culture does.

What culture does:

It supports the advancement of our lives – personal and professional

- It allows for the development of our capabilities
- It facilitates our best possibilities
- It shapes our vision
- It molds our hopes, fears, ambitions, attitudes and actions
- It inspires our dreams for a fulfilling life for future generations and ourselves.

In short, culture is the very ground on which our being develops and evolves.

We can borrow the language of fairy tales and note that if that culture is one that does not nurture or support, where princesses must kiss frogs, i.e., it is one that is:

- not advancing our lives
- not allowing for the development of our capabilities
- not facilitating our best possibilities
- not shaping our best vision for life and work
- not molding our best hopes, ambitions, attitudes, and actions and
- not inspiring our dreams for a fulfilling life for ourselves and future generations,

---

[10] The author is indebted for this image to Page Glennie at the United States Department of the Navy.

14 *Culture, Work and the Knowledge Age*

then transforming the frog into a prince becomes a matter of some urgency. Something must be done.

The Herculean task of changing the form of the cultural framework of our lives is why we turn to myth and tale – they take us as close to Hercules and other cultural heroes as we are likely to get.

In the remaining chapters of this book, we will make much of what myth and fairy tale can teach the modern age about the nature of transformation. Because values are at the heart of culture, let's take a brief look at the tales[11] on which we draw in this book and what values they espouse or warn us against.

Values that tales encourage us to incorporate into our lives

Value	Myth or Tale	Comments
Collaboration	Rumpelstiltskin	The community works together (collaborates) to find the name of the funny little man who is demanding that the Queen give up the land's next ruler, her baby – this saves the kingdom.
Respect for differences	Beauty and the Beast	Beauty learns to look beyond the superficial differences and love/respect the Beast.
Risk-taking	Little Red Riding Hood	Rather than stick to the straight and narrow as instructed by Mother, Little Red strays off the path, meets the wolf, is put into dire straits, but in the end is wiser – she grows up.
Trust	Jack and the Beanstalk	Jack trusts that the beans for which he trades his cow are magical and is rewarded with the hen that lays the perpetual golden egg
Love of Adventure	Ulysses	Ulysses was called beyond the confines of his normal life and stepped through that threshold not only willingly but taking with him a band of co-adventurers – and was rewarded at the end with the love of a faithful wife and devotion of a long-abandoned son.

---

[11] A thumbnail sketch of the tales can be found in Appendix I, in alphabetical order.

| Using one's creativity | Hansel and Gretel | Hansel rose to the occasion of a cruel abandonment by taking what was at hand (breadcrumbs, stones) and using the ordinary in unexpected ways – creating markers for a safe return.
Gretel, knowing the witch planned to eat them both when they were fattened, used a chicken bone to trick the witch into thinking she was still just "skin-and-bones." |

Values tales warn against

Bragging	Rumpelstiltskin	The miller's need to look good in the King's eyes put his daughter's life in danger. Rumpel's gloating revealed his name and was ultimately his undoing.
Hoarding of information	Rumpelstiltskin	Rumpel's power depended on the community not knowing who he was, how he worked – when they found him out, he self-destructed.
Jealousy (feeling threatened by youth)	Snow White	The queen was so threatened by the beauty of her young daughter (the boss was so threatened by the new generation) that she sought the daughter's death, but brought about her own destruction, instead.
Greed	The Fisherman and his Wife	The wife's insatiable greed resulted in the destruction of all the wealth granted by the magic fish.
Short-sightedness	Hansel and Gretel	The stepmother, who can see only the current famine, took the drastic step of abandoning her children and was dead by the time they returned triumphant.

The astute reader familiar with the cultures' tales has realized by now that there are many other values highlighted in myth and tales.[12] These are but a few and are mostly focused on values that translate into the workplace, since this is a book using myth and tales to talk about transforming the work culture.

Having seen the values that ancient wisdom recommends and cautions against, and defined the work culture, let's get a glimpse of where we are going: into the Knowledge Age.

The Knowledge Age

Ours is increasingly known as the Knowledge Age. Today parts of whole industries (management science, information sciences, business improvement technologies, to mention only a few) are now captivated by what is called Knowledge Management. We have created a new class of worker, the Knowledge Worker. Ken Megill argues that, in fact, most workers in developed countries have now become Knowledge Workers.[13] He uses a wonderful example of a worker who, on the face of it, is a manual laborer and makes a convincing argument that, in fact, this is a knowledge worker:

Nothing seems more like work than digging a ditch – it is physical and it is hard. Thinking seems to be the last attribute we might look for in getting a good ditch dug.

However, if you dig ditches for a living today, the way you do that work is likely very different from what it was only a few years ago when you were handed a shovel and told to use your strong back. Today, a ditch digger sits high atop an expensive and complicated piece of machinery. The digger sits in the cabin, which may be air-conditioned. There is probably a computer screen in the cabin that shows the exact requirements for the ditch that needs to be dug. The vast machine is manipulated by an array of knobs and buttons – or, perhaps, by touching a screen that sends directions to the computer that tells the machine what to do.

The work of this professional ditch digger is the same as the man and woman who was handed a shovel and told to move

---

[12] Many more of which are detailed in the chapter on Equipping for the Journey, Section 5, Chapter 10.
[13] Megill, op. cit.

dirt and make a long hole. The work is the same, but the tasks, the qualifications, and expectations of the ditch digger running a computerized back-hoe are very different. The professional ditch-digger needs lots of knowledge and his job is to make judgments – to be certain that the machine is functioning properly, that the proposed ditch is appropriate and that there are no unforeseen obstacles in the way.

The job is to be sure that the hole is "properly" dug and that the machines run "correctly" in doing that job. A ditch is still being dug, but now by a knowledgeable and qualified operator – a knowledge worker who is paid to determine if it is a good idea to dig that ditch there.

The knowledgeable ditch digger works collaboratively as part of a team of other knowledgeable people, many of whom he or she may never meet. Some of those knowledgeable folks have developed plans that include the ditch, perhaps as part of a larger project, but the ditch digger is expected to make adjustments to the plan if the situation at the site indicates.

The leader of the project of which the digging of the ditch is a part of the work needs to respect the knowledge of the ditch digger – and expect the ditch digger to use judgment when doing the work.

But in the end, it is up to the ditch digger to make certain that it is good idea to do what needs to be done and that the computer and the machine properly does what he has decided that they should do. In order to do the work of ditch digging today, the worker needs to understand lots of things. He or she needs to be a knowledge worker.[14]

We argue that The Age of Knowledge, with its culture that supports all workers becoming effective Knowledge Workers, is an age still struggling to be born. It is struggling against the confines of the rules of the old culture; struggling against the common sense of that culture, the "way things are" of that culture. For the birth of this new Knowledge Age to be successful, the culture must change in profound ways in order to support the new work.

The computer, one of the prime enablers of the birth of the Knowledge Age, is simply one of the last new machines of the Industrial Age and fits more or less comfortably into the Industrial Age culture, a culture where

---

[14] Megill, p. 13–14

machines replace the tedious work of humans. It is a culture where work was broken into smaller and smaller pieces.

In the Knowledge Age, though, the reverse is true, each worker must see, know, and integrate larger and larger pieces of the whole picture. Each worker must know the mission of the organization and where he or she fits into that picture. Workers are valued for the knowledge they use, make, and share with their communities of practice. We can see nascent examples of this in the operation of modern warfare, in the scientific community, in cutting edge industries where communities of practice are developed, encouraged, and rewarded and in the operation of modern hospitals, to mention only a few.

Making Knowledge

Many of us have come kicking and screaming into an admission that our work has become the making of Knowledge. That is to say, it is our job to take information created as a result of the work of others, sort through an often overwhelming amount, organize it, compare it to what we know, and make sense of it while guarding against drowning in the overload. We then stack it up against our own experience, apply our own unique set of skills to it, see it through the particular set of lenses we and the organization wear at the moment, and make decisions of the nature "is it a good idea to . . .?" When we answer questions like this, we are creating knowledge. When we share that knowledge with others, they repeat the process we've just been through. In their process our knowledge becomes a piece of the information they sort through, organize, compare, etc. to reach their own conclusions about "is it a good idea to . . .?"

Creating knowledge today is often, but not always, reliant on technology to deliver the latest and most relevant information to us – which is why techno-phobes have entered the Age kicking and screaming. Technology can intimidate, make us feel stupid and incompetent, and leave us feeling impotent, sometimes because of the state of the technology that is still in process. Often, though, it is intimidating because we have been using the new tools in an old culture. Like the maiden in Rumpelstiltskin, we may be locked in the King's storeroom/workplace with a machine we are supposed to know how to use (the spinning wheel/computer) but are now being asked to use it for a new purpose, to make it produce gold (knowledge) not thread (information).

To create knowledge, we must have reliable, timely access to the information we need to do our work. This assumes that we know what our work is, i.e., what it is we do that moves the company or organization toward its mission. It further assumes that we know what information is needed to do that work, what information is created in doing the work and what communities we depend on for getting the information we need and sharing the knowledge we create.

Knowledge work depends on a community of practice[15], it is a collaborative activity (which is essentially social – co-laboring, working together) and it requires new assumptions about how work is done – i.e., it requires a work culture transformation.

A Shared Culture of Knowledge

Knowledge work, as we have seen, is collaborative in nature. It is shared. In order to understand how knowledge is created and how knowledge is shared, we need to look at the concept of community of practice.

Communities, as we use the term, are groups of people who work for a common purpose within an organization, or across organizational boundaries. The community is an environment in which work takes place. Such communities are not restricted to a geographical area, but are connected by their common history and work goals.

. . . Knowledge work is the creative process that gives us answers to questions – "Is it a good idea to . . . ?" These answers are judgments – and if we claim that they are knowledge statements, then we have what philosophers call a "justified true belief."

The work to come to our judgments and beliefs takes place within communities. These communities may be highly formal with settled and organized bodies of knowledge or they may be informal communities with little structured bodies of knowledge. Knowledge management theorists and practitioners call these communities of practice – communities united by a common work and a body of knowledge.

Knowledge arises not out of the particular activity of one person, but the collective work of the community. The conditions for collaboration are created in communities of practice. Of course,

---

[15] The author is indebted to Etienne Wenger for an understanding of communities of practice. For more information, see Wenger, E., McDermott, R. & Snyder, W. Cultivating Communities of practice: A Guide to Managing Knowledge. Boston: Harvard Business School. 2002.

an individual is the source of knowledge, but the development of a body of knowledge and how any particular part of that body fits with the whole, takes place within a community. Knowledge is not just a piece, but part of a whole picture of reality.

Ken Megill, **Thinking for a Living**, p. 108–109.

What would a work culture appropriate for knowledge work look like? Feel like? How does it function? Let us imagine for a moment that we have fully entered the Age of Knowledge – that Age that we can imagine, just around the corner. We can glimpse parts of it, we can feel it on a good day, almost touch it when things go right. Let's step fully into it and describe it.

Characteristics of a Culture of Knowledge

Immediate access

The common sense that workers now bring to work and around which they build their work rituals is that the information they need to complete a day's work is immediately at hand. It is not buried in a morass of useless and overwhelming other data. They know how to find it, where to find it, and access to it is easy.

Over the shoulder in a virtual workplace

Workers work in a transparent workspace. When colleagues need information, they can access the latest knowledge without the creator having to find it, copy it, change its format to meet the colleagues' needs, and send it off. All the workers' reports are handled in this manner. Those who need the report to do their work are given the web site location for it and granted access to it.[16]

Working in a network of communities

Workers engaged in solving similar problems collaborate on answering the myriad "is it a good idea to . . ." sorts of questions surrounding those problems. They know each other, trust each other, work together to solve problems similar in nature.

---

[16] For a delightful reminder of where our culture of hoarded values originates, see Noel Dickover's essay in Appendix 4. Even if you're not normally an appendix reader, this one is worth the effort.

Web-enabled technology takes over much of the tedium

Much of what workers found tedious in the Information Age can now be handled by technology. Meetings need not involve travel. Filing documents, forms, claims – all the tedium of secretarial office work – can be handled electronically. Important knowledge is stored and sorted for future use; its use monitored by those responsible for and especially trained to deal with corporate memory.

Changes in attitude

Workers and bosses alike have discovered that there is nothing magical about beginning work at 8 or 9 and ending at 5, or 6, or 7. We find and make answers to burning questions and un-knot the thorniest problems at the oddest times, from the oddest places. The value a knowledge worker adds to the work is not harnessed to a 9–5 schedule.

Telecommuting

Nor is our productivity, thinking, or problem-solving tied to sitting in an office at a desk. Because workers can be in touch with the community or network of communities through an integrated digital environment,[17] there is no need for workers' bodies to be at a particular office, at a particular time.

Intuition over Sensation

Through the Industrial Age and into the early stages of the Information Age, the dominant personality preference of the people of the Western world was Sensation (as opposed to Intuition).[18] The sensation function is that part of the personality that relies on things that can be seen, felt, smelled, and measured. It is responsible for our noticing the specifics as opposed to the larger picture, the facts as opposed to the ideas, the practical as opposed to the innovative, and the history as opposed to the possibilities.

---

[17] See Appendix IV for a fuller discussion of an Integrated Digital Environment.
[18] Myers Briggs Type Inventory (MBTI) measures a person's preferences among four personality functions: Introversion/Extroversion; Sensation/Intuition; Thinking/Feeling and Perception/Judgment. Research reveals that 75% of people tested show a preference for Sensation over Intuition. For more information on the Myers Briggs Type Inventory, see Keirsey, D and D.W., and Bates, M. Please Understand Me. Del Mar, CA: Prometheus Nemesis, 1978.

When the Knowledge Age arrives, intuition and creativity will be more highly valued than it was in the industrial world. Those with vision and ideas, willing to try something with no precedent, will be in the forefront of making knowledge. To be sure, the sensation function is vital to the process, but intuition will be prized for its quick insight into the possibilities of new solutions. Who knows? Perhaps with the new reliance on and valuing of the other function, it will dominate in the psyches of knowledge workers.

Adventure

Change in the workplace has often been equated with the chaos of redrawing communication lines, downsizing, and reorganization. But when people know how to equip for the journey of transformation, change can be seen as an adventure. No longer do monsters inhabit the part of the earth that lies past the known. And dragons can be slain with the arrows, chased with the horses, and guarded against with the robes and armor the hero knows to take on the journey.[19]

Thinking

In the Knowledge Age, thinking for a living becomes the norm. Those who believe that they simply make widgets or dig ditches, in fact, are valued for their knowledge. They know where to get what they need to do their work, collaborate with others involved in widget-making and ditch digging, make their knowledge available to others who need it to do their work. They, like their colleagues in a high-technology firm dedicated to providing the latest knowledge to scientists, are knowledge workers in the Knowledge Age.

How do we get there from here?

Computers can perform much of the tedious work, so what does this free humans to do? Many would answer: "To make and use knowledge." Modern businesses see their knowledge as their cutting edge. How do we usher in the Age of Knowledge? Perhaps it would be better to ask how do we cooperate with the transformation that is knocking at the door?[20]

---

[19] See Chapter 10 for a discussion of other equipment for the hero on the journey.
[20] As we discuss later in the Hero's Journey, we will see that we do have a choice about answering the door, or not – though the fate of heroes who decline the call to adventure is not an interesting or exciting one. They are doomed to lives of restrictive safety, boredom, and sameness; or in mythical language, they live in the kingdom where the king and all crops are dying, life is poor, and threats from outside abound.

If we are to undertake a transformation of the work culture, we are better equipped to succeed if we are forewarned that transformation is a process that is not neat, controllable, and predictable. The outcome will be a culture we do not recognize, a New World on the other side of the terra incognita into which profound change throws us. Most of us are attached to the illusion that we are in perfect control of our lives, the masters of our own fate. We might well ask, "Why would anyone in his/her right mind willingly throw him/herself into what appears to the left brain to be the deeply unsettling chaos of terra incognita?" Why, indeed, would a learned person who has studied the earlier transformation from one age to another willingly initiate another such transformation?

> **Agrarian to Industrial**
>
> The transformation from the Agrarian Age to the Industrial Age was one that changed the form of the work lives of most human beings. No longer did they work their own fields, create their own meals, shelter, clothing. They now collected into cities where factories made the commodities the farm once produced. The very assumptions that these new factory workers brought with them to work changed. Their ideas about time (work time/free time) and production changed, as did their beliefs and values about relationships with workers, bosses, and the workplace. In short, this was a work culture transformation – the form of work that they used to know was no longer recognizable. (Some viewed this as a frog-to-prince type change, others were convinced that the prince had been enchanted into a frog.) Each shift from Age to Age brought with it similar paradigm shifts about reality – these shifts in "the common sense," the "what everyone knows" of work we are calling work culture transformations. As we leave the Information Age and enter the Knowledge Age the culture change will be as profound as that shift from the Agrarian to the Industrial Age.

The answer, of course, is that we don't willingly initiate it. Life has dealt it to us. We have been or are being hit by the cosmic two-by-four.[21] Because we are at the beginning of this new work age we cannot know its final form, but we do know many things about how transformations happen in personal lives and that knowledge of the transformative process can inform how we enter this new culture.

---

[21] For those not familiar with American jargon, a two-by-four is a standard building board 2 inches deep and 4 inches wide. The "cosmic" two-by-four may well be 2 feet deep by 4 feet wide, or at least it feels that way when it hits one's life.

Armed with (1) information about how transformations are made, (2) a sharply focused lens for seeing the process, and (3) a new language to articulate it, one can lead and shape the transformation, not fall victim to it. A leader with such knowledge will prepare the workforce for the transformation, increase profits and productivity, and place him or herself on the forefront of a new business culture that may mystify and elude others.

What will happen depends on many things, both for a person and an organization. Sometimes external factors – earthquakes, fires, pestilence – will determine what happens. Sometimes acts of other nations or cultures may determine what happens: globalization, terrorism, or war, for example.

But what happens also depends on us and how we choose to live our lives. Do we see a major upheaval in life, a complete disruption, as a call to the journey, a call to transcend the old worn-out patterns? Or do we see ourselves as victims of fate, impotent to shape our responses? This is not to suggest that we get to live however we wish – even in the very best fairy tale the "happy ever after" only comes after lots of turmoil and heartbreak. And it is only a short while before the next chapter, a new tale, begins.

It is this turmoil that interests us, though – the turmoil of transformation. It is the making of a new work culture out of the old.

We believe that the transformation of our society that is going on all about us should be embraced and welcomed – and we should seek to shape this transformation to make it as humane and life-giving as possible. To do so, we must understand transformation and the role of the hero, i.e., each one of us, in it.

SECTION II

The Modern Hero

In which we talk about different aspects of the hero and heroing.

Who? Me? A hero?

Many people with whom we've spoken about the ideas in this book have objected to seeing themselves as heroes: it seems too grandiose. Heroes, after all, are like King Arthur, or Ulysses, or Psyche, or Hera, Babe Ruth, New York firefighters, Mohandas Gandhi, or Bishop Tutu – people of outstanding courage or ability, admired for bravery or nobility, models for others to follow. I agree that both ancient heroes and modern are writ larger than life. Many heroes (those that are not gods) begin life as quite ordinary people. It is because of their attitudes and actions while on the journey that they have been immortalized in the world's literature. Most of us will not be discovered and canonized in world literature. Those who undertake the journey of transformation today are, however, nonetheless heroes – with the courage, bravery and nobility attendant to heroes old and new. They also are models for others – for their children, grandchildren, neighbors, and colleagues. Those who recognize that the extraordinary struggles to overcome adversity make them the hero of their own lives may have less difficulty with the concept of Everyman as Hero.

This book expands the conviction that personal transformation is a hero's journey into the conviction that work culture transformation is also a hero(es)' journey. Those who would accept the call to transformation of a workplace traverse the same territory as heroes from the dawn of time. There is only one journey.

Heroes are people who take that journey. They are people who, when presented the opportunity to transform, take up the challenge – answer the call to adventure with a "yes!" – Either resounding and enthusiastic, or hesitating and reluctant. One way or another, they set out on the hero's journey.

There are, of course heroes writ large and small. Joseph Campbell[22] articulates it nicely when he says:

---

[22] Joseph Campbell died in 1987 but left behind the definitive body of work on myth and its relationship to psychology. For example, he pointed out themes that are repeated in myths of every culture and drew parallels with modern cultures. For readers wishing more depth, see: Campbell: The Hero with a Thousand Faces. Princeton. Princeton University, 1973. Campbell's work was based on C.G. Jung's earlier research into world mythologies.

> *"Typically, the hero of the fairy tale achieves a domestic, microcosmic triumph, and the hero of a myth a world-historical, macrocosmic triumph . . ."[23]*

The hero writ large brings back from the journey the means to regenerate the society.

---

[23] Campbell, Joseph. Hero with a Thousand Faces. Princeton: Princeton University, 1973, p. 37.

CHAPTER 2

Heroes

In which we introduce the characteristics of heroes.

We have not to risk the adventure alone, for the heroes of all time have gone before us. The labyrinth is thoroughly known. . . . And where we had thought to be alone, we will be with all the world.
– Joseph Campbell, The Hero with a Thousand Faces, p. 25.

Modern day heroes

Few of us think of ourselves as heroes. But this is a book for and about heroes, the heroes who are ordinary folks like you and me. Folks who are, for some reason or other, faced with the possibility of a transformation (thrust into an extraordinary situation) – and go through it (rise to the occasion). Caterpillars face the necessity of a transformation through another stage of chrysalis to become butterflies; the essential difference between them and a hero is that caterpillars have no choice. Unfortunately (it seems sometimes) human beings do; they must make a difficult choice to complete a transformation. (Put one foot in front of the other and do the best next thing that has to be done.)

So, yes, it is possible that you are the modern hero about to make a journey – you may even be part way down the road on that journey, caught in the jaws of change. You may not even want this journey, but you may not have a choice because the world in which you are living is becoming one where knowledge, not industry, is our dominant resource. We are entering into the Knowledge Age – leaving the last stage of the

Industrial Age, the Information Age, behind us. This is a journey of some distance and some difficulty, a journey of transformation. A journey to a new way to do work … a new work culture appropriate for this Knowledge Age.[24]

What heroes do and have always done

- They see the opportunity behind a cataclysmic disruption of life
- They cross the threshold from the known world to the unknown, and wander
- They accept help from unusual sources.
- They return triumphant with a treasure.

These four distinct actions constitute the journey: make your own fairy-tale.

As you may have noticed, our heroes are sometimes very un-heroic. In fact, if you look at most heroes, they don't strut around shouting about their heroism.

They go about their lives and do what needs to be done. They do the right thing when others do the easy thing or the thing that will bring immediate gratification. In fact, a typical hero has the key characteristics that will epitomize the worker in the Knowledge Age.[25] A hero is unselfish and sharing, someone who makes information available to others, knowing that the information will grow as others use it and be of even more value to the hero. For information does not dissipate with sharing. This is the essential attitude that underlies the work culture that is appropriate for the Knowledge Age.

Trust is part and parcel of the sharing attitude of the hero, trusting others to deal with you in a way that makes sense to them (if not to you). Trust does not require the hero to be naïve, but does expect an attitude of openness to prevail and infuse the work and life of the hero.

For in the end (and the beginning, but not always in the middle), the hero is a pretty ordinary person who gets up in the morning and makes

---

[24] "The essence of heroism always involves taking a journey into the unknown and bringing some sort of knowledge out of the unknown that benefits either society or an organization. The hero brings new prosperity to the organizational wasteland." Wahlstrom, Tomi Lennart. Psychological Applications in Management: The Hero's Journey. 1996. Unpublished doctoral dissertation, Colorado Technical University, Colorado Springs.

[25] More about these characteristics in Equipping for the Journey, Section V, Chapter 10.

it through the day. But instead of going to work, putting in the eight hours and coming home to have free time, the hero takes a sense of adventure with him throughout life. The hero is a professional – a pro at living and experiencing and, above all, at questioning and being willing to take help from unexpected places and people.

The hero can be every man and every woman. What makes the hero different is the call to adventure and the response that comes in stepping across the threshold of the known into the wilderness.

Here is how one expert on heroes puts it, speaking of the many myths and heroes of history:

It (is and) will be always the one, shape-shifting yet marvelously constant story that we find, together with a challengingly persistent suggestion of more remaining to be experienced than will ever be known or told.[26]

When people make a personal transformation – one that changes the form of their personality – they follow the path that heroes of old followed. The same process can apply to organizations undergoing the transformation of their work culture. The journey and the process are one.

Organizations as individuals

Organizations come in many forms: companies, partnerships, corporations, non-profits, government, and military, to name but a few. Corporations are already treated as individuals under U.S. law. Other organizational forms, too, can be seen as individuals, psychologically, if not legally. Since the middle twentieth century there has been a psychological discipline called organizational behavior. There is an International Society for the Psychoanalytic Study of Organizations that held its 1997 symposium at a respected graduate school of business. It can even be argued that organizations have egos.[27] Organizations also have personalities (cultures) and are spoken of as dysfunctional (having a pathology) when they are not operating efficiently. All of these concepts are borrowed from psychology, a scientific discipline founded to explore what makes individuals "tick." For other examples, see living systems theory, a theory that

---

[26] Campbell, op. cit. p.3.
[27] "Ego" was just Freud's way of giving a scientific sounding name to "I," i.e., that part of the personality one identifies with – says "this is who I am."

demonstrates how organizations and people have a lot of the same basic processes and systems in common.[28]

The missing road map

One reality for the hero and the hero's journey is that there is no road map. One can't go to the map store and ask for an off-the-shelf guide for this journey; there is no three-step process. For managers, workers, planners, and those of us who are used to thinking in terms of road maps and project design and implementation, the chapter on equipping for the journey provides an approach to leadership for the journey into the Knowledge Age. The new equipment provides capabilities that come from the whole-picture, stories and metaphors part of our brains. This equipment complements the planning, managing, designing and implementing part of the brain. How fascinating to use both parts – the whole of our brains.

Embracing transformation

While I was in my psychotherapist incarnation, working with people toward transformation, nearly everyone who came to my consulting room spent a great deal of life's energy bemoaning the fact that life does not come with a road map. However, if we have the spirit of adventure appropriate for transformation, we find that when given a road map, the only self respecting thing to do is to look at it, learn what we can from it and then ignore it and create our own map. Or, at best we use a map as a guide rather than a reference. Time spent in search of a road map is time not spent on the journey. Most of us create a map that outlines the journey we have individually embraced; often our maps are made retrospectively to examine a journey we have, in reality, already taken. It is often only in looking back that we can see our way clearly. Each time we re-invent ourselves, we re-draw our road map. It is always a work in progress.

In my career of training and sometimes re-training therapists not to be mechanics who "fix" dysfunctional personalities, but to be explorers and co-creators of lives-as-works-of-art, one of my most daunting tasks was to help them to throw away their concepts of an off-the-shelf road map.

---

[28] Miller, James Grier. Living Systems Theory. New York: McGraw Hill, 1978.

If budding therapists (or experienced ones, for that matter) began a session thinking that they knew the right destination, they had become again therapist-as-mechanic – someone there to fix a problem; someone who thinks in a reductionistic way that says: "one problem, one cause, one solution. Oh, and by the way, I am the expert and I can fix it."

A hero's journey cannot be reduced to a simple one-to-one relationship of cause to effect. The journey does not lend itself to reduction.

Reductionism

Reductionism is the view that a complex problem can be traced back to a specific cause. It is the foundation of modern science. It is what separates the hard sciences from the "soft" ones. Systems theory field is a reaction against the philosophy of reductionism because when you reduce something into its smallest parts, you lose an understanding of how the whole works.

Freud's belief that adult neuroses largely stem from childhood sexual issues can be seen as reductionistic. What a reductionistic stance means for the psychologists-as-mechanic is that we analyze the problem, find one historical wound that "caused" it and set forth a plan of action to "fix" it. We ask, "where did this problem originate? What is its source?" We faithfully follow the problem back to its inception, "fix" it at its point of inception and test the "fix" against today's reality to see if it works.

This is a fine approach as far as it goes. Certainly, repairing an unsatisfactory relationship, for example, is a worthy endeavor. Analyzing a problem, planning a way to repair it or to work around it, is a great beginning. It is enough to make life immediately better, make it work more smoothly, efficiently, effectively. But that is not enough to make of life an Opus, a work of art – something worthy of spending one's precious, irreplaceable lifetime doing. It does not effect a transformation. Transformation is a creative act, more like painting, choreographing a dance, or writing an opera than following directions.

A powerful therapist, like a powerful leader, is an artist, one who helps others tap the excitement and mystery of life, a mythic-explorer. Leaders and followers alike who would be the artist of their own Magnum Opus of life and work must do as heroes do:

- See what others call catastrophic as a call to the hero's journey, an opportunity
- Accept the call, even though it means leaving the comfort of the known
- Struggle with strange adversaries, battle unknown monsters, and accept

help from a few who will offer it
- Return to the world they left, renewed, energetic, transformed and make the world a better place.

It is the same journey heroes have always taken and embodies the same stages that heroes of old underwent, most often kicking and screaming, dragged by life, fate, the gods, or circumstances beyond their control into their role as hero.

Beyond reductionism: adding art

The thoughts, the "voices," of ancient cultures as they sought to make sense of the world around them and their place in it come to us through their myths and tales – the creation of which is a collective artistic endeavor. Using those myths and tales to help understand today's problems universalizes an individual problem and adds the essential ingredient needed to make one's life a work of art. Using myth and tales about the mother-child relationship, for example, puts the modern problem in perspective. It is no longer just this particular person trying to find a way to a mature relationship with this particular Mother. It is a struggle, an initiation, that has happened to every child in every culture in every age as the childhood relationship with Mother is transformed into an adult one. Today's particular relationship now stands as part of a rich tapestry of history – a part of the great art of humankind.

Each of us who rises to the occasion of transformation is a hero. In fact, the rising to the occasion is the same mental attitude that allows us to see life's disruptions as a call to change – one that we know will not be easy. We know that we won't find one root of one problem that will put us back into the good old days – that's not even what we want. But if we are open to receiving help from unexpected sources, we trust that at the other end something good will emerge.

CHAPTER 3

The Hero's Transformation

In which we lay the groundwork for the hero's actions later in the book.

Looking at these Dead White Western Men may seem like a strange detour in our discussion of work culture transformation. But bear with me, if you will, for they will be giving us some of the tools that we need to understand how we can become heroes and accept the adventurous transformation coming our way. What follows is a brief overview of their ideas.

Idea 1. An active and creative approach to problem solving saves years on the "analyst's couch" and gives deep insight into the whole picture.[29]

Idea 2. Human beings go through transformation many times in the process of living life successfully.[30]

Idea 3. Transformation is a journey – it meanders through swamps and scales mountains, it does not go in the straightest line from point A to point B.[31]

Idea 4. Journeys of transformation follow the pattern of the hero's journey.[32]

Idea 5. Across cultures, there is only one journey.[33]

Idea 6. Myths and fairy tales illustrate the components, the stages, of the journey.[34]

---

[29] A contribution of J.L. Moreno.
[30] A contribution from the study of Carl Jung.
[31] Another Jungian idea.
[32] A contribution from Joseph Campbell.
[33] Another Campbell contribution.
[34] From Jung and Campbell.

- Myths and tales had an important role for ancient and not-so-ancient societies.
- These myths and the transformation that heroes go through in these myths were not just entertaining stories, but they taught lessons from which everyone – ancient and modern – could learn.
- Modern individuals (modern heroes), too, can make sense of their world and transform themselves by understanding myths in a modern context.
- Organizations can also transform themselves and their work culture by embracing/supporting the hero's journey as an organization.

Idea 7. Rumpelstiltskin is an excellent example of a fairy tale that has significance to us today because it involves both individual and group transformation, and it teaches lessons that are especially important in today's context of the knowledge workplace.[35]

Three of the great thinkers from the *fin de siècle* Viennese salons come to our aid in conceptualizing the transformation process. Jung tells us that life itself is a journey from immaturity to maturity. Campbell adds that the tales of old have always spoken about this journey, and if we examine them, they will guide us. Moreno says "Put it in action – play it out and find your own individual way to be a hero in your own life."

Joseph Levy Moreno (1889–1974) and psychodrama

J.L. Moreno developed a method that demands both right and left brain effort in solving problems, a method that is at once practical and lyrical. We introduce him first, though he entered the scene after Jung, because his methodology can bring to life, by utilizing the setting of stage and drama, the whole picture of Jung and Campbell's work.

Joseph Moreno was part of the heady mix of intellectuals who inhabited turn-of-the-century Vienna. That Age ended with World War I and the culture transformation resulting from the fall of the great European monarchies. The Viennese salons of that time were the Paris of later years and the New York of more recent years. Vienna was where music, art, ideas, and creativity were blossoming. Moreno was a contemporary of both Freud and Jung, who were also part of Viennese salons of that time.

---

[35] A contribution for which only the author can be blamed.

Moreno developed a practical, social psychology while his colleagues Freud and Jung were theorizing about the function of the unseen, unknown, and unknowable influences on the psyche. Moreno integrated his love of the theatre and his experience of the influence of the roles people play in life into his approach to psychotherapy. This approach he called psychodrama.

Psychodrama is a group therapy methodology that employs techniques of the theatre in the service of therapy. The client becomes the playwright/protagonist, and personal problems become the stuff of the play. Group members become the actors in the protagonist's production. The psychotherapist, trained in the methods of psychodrama, becomes the play's director.

Like any good theatre, the success of the psychodrama depends on the protagonist's – and the director's – creativity. It depends on their ability to see the larger context of the problem, to universalize it and to make of it high art, to make it sing, dance and move and in the process to involve the audience in the experience.

In the end the solution to any problem presented by the protagonist must pass the "so what" test: what difference will this make in the quality of my life?

One of the jobs of the director is to enrich and help universalize the themes of the play so that the protagonist's life struggles become the stuff of the Magnum Opus of the protagonist's (and others') lives.[36] No play that does not transcend its own boundaries lasts long on Broadway. To be a long-running classic, it must be universal – it must go beyond a particular protagonist with a particular problem.

Moreno focused much of his energy on helping people define the "socius" (the bonds of friendship) in which they live. He developed sociometry, the measure of those bonds, which he applied in World War I refugee camps, as a means to help refugees create a tolerable situation. To this study, he added role theory and his assertion that through the various roles into which we are thrust and those we create for ourselves in life, we are co-creators of the world in which we live.

Thus was born psychodrama.[37] The tools and the results of psychodrama, which I used and achieved in my own practice, taught me

---

[36] If the protagonist can do this for himself he does not bring the problem to the psychodrama stage for solution.

[37] For more information see Blatner, Adam. Acting in: Practical applications of psychodramatic methods. New York: Springer. 1988; and Williams, Anthony. The Passionate technique: Strategic psychodrama with individuals, families, and groups. London: Tavistock/Routledge. 1989. While both of these books are less than current, they are seminal.

the importance of decisions and the vital necessity of taking action, of saying "yes!" to the journey of transformation when the call comes, whether on a personal or on a social level.

Carl Jung (1875–1961) and analytical psychology

Carl Jung identified patterns/elements of society that have meaning across cultures and across ages. He demonstrates a universal dimension to current issues and challenges.

The analytical psychology of Carl Jung focuses on integrating all parts of the personality into a whole. The movement from an immature personality to a mature one involves a shifting of the control of the psyche from the Ego to the Self.[38] The process of this maturation he called individuation – beginning to stand as an individual not defined by the limitations of parents or society, but defined by the deeper understanding of one's inner being and its relationship to the outer world.

Jung visited many cultures, collecting their myths and folk tales in an attempt to compare the ways people understand the world in which they live. He concluded that certain mythic themes/patterns repeat in each culture and that we are more alike across cultures than we are different. These repeating themes, constant from culture to culture, he called archetypes.

The goal of the analytical psychology of Jung goes beyond solving the immediate problem. Like a butterfly the psyche[39] gathers nectar from many many flowers. The soul, like the butterfly, can never, while it has life, be pinned down or reduced to one cause or repaired with one solution.

Exploring the psyche in its relationship to an archetypical Mother (for example) unvarying from culture to culture, gives people a new place to stand, an enlarged point of view. It gives them a larger, older, wiser perception of the "problem" they are having with their particular Mother. It makes them a part of the ancient deep-rooted community of Humankind.

A particular person's problem, situation, or conundrum is not just a personal one arising out of the particular problem that, for example, a particular mother and a particular child have, but is an instance, a continuing example, of a much greater and more profound fact of life – an archetype. By exploring problems in this manner, we have gone far beyond solving the immediate situation.

---

[38] For definition of Ego and Self, see Appendix II.
[39] In Greek, psyche means not only soul but also butterfly.

When a psychotherapist shifts from solving immediate social problems to focusing on psyche, wholeness is the goal. To be whole is to integrate the parts of the personality of which we are aware and to know and relate to those parts of the personality of which we are not conscious – but make themselves known to us through dreams, stories, feelings, and our acts of creativity.

Understanding our wholeness solves more problems than reducing them to a cause and effect relationship. For example, a male client appeared in my consulting room with a problem with his boss that seemed insurmountable and would likely terminate my client's job. Reducing the problem to a similarity between boss and Dad could lead to *some* resolution of the problem: improved communication with both, understanding of why the boss "pushed his buttons," and some clarity about other bosses in his history. Placing the problem in the context of the archetype of the Shadow allowed the client to see the aspect of himself that was activated when he was in contact with either Dad or the boss. He could see how he was like the part of each of them that he disliked and to which he reacted negatively. He had a more universal understanding not only about their problem, but about his own, larger personality, as well. His personality now had room for a tolerance of more of his wholeness; some of his shadow had been integrated into his self-understanding.

A similar example occurred with a female client who entered therapy because of difficulty finding more satisfying work. During our work together, she had recurring dreams about a dark, threatening male standing in her doorway; each night he seemed more menacing and closer. She tried to liken him to males she had known, but had no moment of recognition, no "aha!" moment, that told her this was the right approach. When she put the figure into the context of the animus, a universal part of the feminine psyche that functions to help her participate in a patriarchal world, she understood some of the difficulties she was having in interview situations. She had enlarged her self-perception to include a part of herself of which she had been unconscious – a part that had, in fact, been threatening her success in the world of interviewing.

To better understand what Jung had in mind, let us take an example from a well-known fairy tale, Hansel and Gretel. If you want to remind yourself of this tale (or any other mentioned along the way), just see Appendix I.

Example: Hansel and Gretel[40] speaks to a child's real fear of abandonment

Children, in the process of transformation into adults, must overcome the fear of abandonment. To do so the children must learn to problem-solve and to rely on themselves and their abilities to think and act in realistic ways. What better way to portray the importance of this task and the difficulties involved than to make a story of it – a story about abandonment in a dark woods at the hands of an evil-intending parent: Hansel and Gretel.

Children see the parents' increasing demand that they learn to stand on their own two feet as an "evil" deprivation of support. They believe that those they could always depend on are now abandoning them (Mom convinces Dad to leave the children in the woods – with only enough food for one meal). This abandonment is frightening (a dark-woods-experience). It must be attempted more than once before success is achieved (the stones and the bread-crumb markers to find the way back into dependency on Mom and Dad).

Before a child successfully learns to problem-solve and become self-reliant there are many wrong choices with potentially life-threatening consequences (a child-eating witch in a deceptive gingerbread house). In the end the children succeed because they are resourceful, depend on each other, think creatively, and act decisively.

Hansel and Gretel is a tale of transformation. Children are called to the great adventure of growing up. Hansel and Gretel's call was delivered by the means of the fearsome abandonment by parents. Their uncharted wilderness is a deep forest full of wild animals and unknown dangers, the worst of which is a witch who, in fact, captures them. Help comes from the younger sister's resourcefulness and quick action – not the place Hansel would expect it to come from. The boon they bring back is the witch's trunk full of treasure.

Theirs was a heroes' journey, for it led the two children from childhood – and dependence – to maturity and independence, the wholeness of childhood. It was a journey of transformation.

---

[40] For a synopsis of the tale, see Appendix I.

Joseph Campbell (1904–1987) and the monomyth

Like Jung, Campbell[41] did extensive research in myths and tales in all the world's cultures. In his formidable body of knowledge, he passed on to us the concept of the Hero's Journey. He discovered and articulated the stages in ancient myth and fairy tales that each of the heroes undergoes. In fact, each hero is every person, thrust into the challenges of life. Every myth is the same story, the monomyth.

Campbell identifies the universal psychological components of myths and fairy tales. He shows us that these stories formulated ages ago have relevance today because they came to grips with the fundamental psychological challenges that face people today just as they did in the past.

Joseph Campbell was a young boy when the ferment of Western Europe on the eve of the First World War produced Freud, Jung, and others who explored the basis for human behavior. By the time Campbell was a young adult, Jung had broken with Freud's reductionistic view that all neuroses could be traced to childhood sexual fantasies or realities. Like Jung, Campbell found deep insights into human behavior by studying the tales and myths of old.

Myths and tales had fascinated Campbell from childhood. Jung's seminal research added to Campbell's enthusiasm. Campbell's studies led him from his home in America to Europe to study in Paris and Munich. Picasso and Matisse were the reigning artists at the time, Thomas Mann was writing and Freud and Jung were at their peak. The colonies of the European powers were restless and representatives of what later became the independence movements throughout the world were learning, studying and living in Europe's cities. New forms of architecture were arising. Social ferment was all around. Campbell was a kid in the candy store.

Campbell returned to the United States, pockets full of candy from the European store. He read several languages – eastern and western, and was convinced that the myths he had always loved are linked to the psyche. That myths embodied psychological truths explained the endurance of myth and tales over the millennia.

Not only do myths speak in symbolic language of the stuff of psychological life, they also are an expression of a universal need to know: to

---

[41] Campbell popularized, for the American public, his view of myth in a television series, The Power of Myth. Bill Moyers, a popular Public Broadcast host, interviewed Campbell for the series, making his work very accessible. The program was televised in 1988 the year after Campbell's death at the age of 83 and is available on video from the Public Broadcast Service.

explain social, spiritual, cosmological realities experienced by humankind. They are the way ancient people explained their world, how they taught their children about life's major events and mysteries.

Campbell lamented the passing of the golden age of myth-making, that age when myths spoke to humans and influenced civilization:

> *We live, today, in a terminal moraine of myths and mythic symbols, fragments large and small of traditions that formerly inspired and gave rise to civilizations.*[42]

To capture that once glorious age, Campbell undertook a comprehensive guide to world myths. This guide traces the history of myth – in an effort to "convert the rubble of the great moraine that is about us into a laboratory of revelations."[43] In the introduction to the first volume he said that two of the functions myths serve are:

- to help individuals capture a sense of wonder and mystery about their world and
- to conduct them in harmony through the stages of life from the dependency of birth and childhood, through old age and death.

Putting Jung and Campbell together

Using the hero's journey as a way of understanding transformation, people in search of deep and lasting change move forward. They do not just make the changes necessary for making life work. They begin to wonder about the meaning of their individual life, to ask and find answers to the question, "Tell me, what is it you plan to do with your one wild and precious life?"[44] These questions move people to deeper discoveries about life, and the answers involve a more profound change: a transformation – a shifting of the center of balance from the ego to the larger, more all-encompassing Self. Self is open to possibilities, takes itself lightly, knows the dark as well as the light, and is a passionate participant in life.

---

[42] Campbell, Joseph. Historical Atlas of World Mythology, Vol. I; The Way of the Animal Powers: Part 1: Mythologies of the Primitive Hunters and Gatherers. New York: Harper & Row, 1988, p.8.
[43] ibid, p. 9
[44] Oliver, Mary. "The Summer Day." In New and Selected Poems. Boston: Beacon Press, 1992.

Campbell and Jung shared a conviction that all myths, tales, and epics are early manifestations of the universal need to explain social, cosmological and spiritual realities. They believed that myths and tales have survived the test of time for the same reason the classics have, because they tell us essential truths about how the world works and what makes people tick. Since the Megalithic period (the era in which Stonehenge was erected) common people have expressed the way they see nature and their societies through tales. As they made new discoveries, they transformed their tales.[45]

Integrating Jung and Campbell's way of seeing the experience of being human provides today's seekers with a template for transformation. Today's denizens undergo transformations in the process of living successful lives no less than the ancients did. In fact, anyone who has faced profound changes and integrated them into his or her life has undertaken the same journey. Heroes have, indeed, a Thousand Faces.[46]

Integrating Jung and Campbell into Moreno's Psychodrama

As a psychotherapist almost every person I saw had the same basic set of psychodramas[47] – the same territory to traverse en route to wholeness. My work showed me that we are all the heroes of our own life's journey (unless we refuse the call to the adventure of that journey and settle in to live "lives of quiet desperation."[48]) My work with clients and patients showed me that the stages of those journeys are no different from those described by Campbell as the hero's journey. Each of us, if we make life's transformation into purpose and wholeness, experiences the same stages of the journey as ancient heroes did.

The integration of Moreno's psychodrama, Jung's analytic psychology, and Campbell's concept of the monomyth, into my own practice brought about a psychotherapy that uses the active, artistic approach of psychodrama with the analytic thinking of Jung and Campbell's under-

---

[45] For more on folk and fairy tales, see Zipes, Jack. Breaking the Magic Spell: Radical Theories of Folk and Fairy Tales. New York: Methuen, 1979.
[46] An allusion to Campbell, Joseph. Hero with a Thousand Faces. Princeton University, 1973.
[47] The classic dramas include ones about Mom, Dad, Time, Birth, Death, God, Love, Children, Sexual orientation, and Learning to live with the world outside the home.
[48] Thoreau, Henry David. Walden; and, Civil Disobedience: Complete Texts with Introduction, Historical Contexts, Critical Essays, edited by Paul Lauter. Boston: Houghton Mifflin: 2000. "The mass of men lead lives of quiet desperation," p. 43.

standing of myth. After training psychodramatists for some time, I found that the psychodramatic methodology, when it embodied only the social psychology on which Moreno based it, was limited. Social psychology addresses only the conscious level of living – those bonds and difficulties formed through the process of living the particular life dealt to us. There is more to each of us than that level of living. And therefore I annexed the concepts of Jung and Campbell to reach deeper levels of psychotherapeutic change.

My practice taught me that en route to wholeness, we are all modern heroes, all of whom are from time to time hit by the cosmic two-by-four, taken out of what we like to think of as our ordinary lives, the lives we control, manage and direct. After such a cosmic concussion, we wander for a time in a wilderness until we learn the way and erect new signposts for behavior. We re-orient to unusual helpers and return to a newly defined ordinary life with a gift that has made our lives better.

The three unlikely bedfellows, Moreno, Jung, and Campbell, make a rich understanding of life – one that is at once active, creative, and curiosity-provoking. The psychotherapist combining these three approaches notes that what they have in common is:

- a respect for the unknown, (loving the lack of a road map),
- an appreciation for the open-endedness of the journey (what's around the next bend in this journey?), and
- a realization that there is no one "right" way for one to live life (except to be alive to possibility, open to a call to adventure.)

Many who come into therapy thinking they want to transform, unfortunately, refuse the call. Many timid-hearted would-be-leaders, many workers who prefer not to be challenged, many sideline-sitters never take the journey, fail to recognize the help offered on the way, or do not make the return trip, bringing the boon back to the community. The journey is not preordained. Success is not guaranteed. It is not for naught that the ancients marked this part of the map "hic sunt animales" – "here be monsters." But those who do decide to go on their own journey of transformation have the wisdom/insights of myths and tales to draw upon.

So now we turn to an investigation of the stages of transformation discovered by these three great men. These stages give us what we need to understand how we can turn straw into gold . . . and accept the call to adventure.

SECTION III

Universal Stages of Transformation

In which we define transformation and outline the journey – as close to a road map as we come – but Rand McNally[49] would never buy it.

---
[49] Rand McNally is one of the largest U.S. map makers

There is a wonderful illustration of transformation in the tadpole's journey to froghood. The Frog to Prince transformation gets all the press but the metamorphosis from tadpole to frog is more impressive and a lot more work. Yes, the frog has to gain a lot of weight, change its coloration and rearrange its facial features to become a prince, but it happens instantaneously. Tadpoles, however, grow legs, lose a tail, reconfigure jaws and digestive tract, change the mode of locomotion, and acquire new food sources.

Transformation in the context of personal life and the work culture is the same sort of profound change the tadpole must undergo to become a frog.[50] It usually involves hard work, pain, and turmoil. Imagine for a moment the tadpole thrown into complete chaos as its world totally changes into one that had been alien: a world where air is a medium for life, where flies are food, where legs let him leap through the air. After a transformation to a new work culture, our world will be just as unrecognizable to our old "tadpole" selves as the bewildered frog's is.

> **Transformation is a shift in how we experience the world**

---

[50] Frog to prince, while just as profound, has none of the sense of hard work and turmoil one can imagine for the tadpole. The frog who becomes prince does so magically and with a kiss from a beautiful woman, no less.

CHAPTER 4

Transformation

In which we amplify the definition of transformation.

Transformation

To transform means to change form. Birth transforms a fetus into an infant. High heat transforms water into steam; freezing temperatures change the same substance into ice. A human being having had a near-death experience often emerges with a fundamentally changed set of values and view of life. Revolution transformed France from a monarchy to a republic.

Transformation in ancient cultures involved rites of initiation, rites of passage. For example, the transformation of boys to men in ancient cultures involved a series of trials. Without these rites of passage, (the successful completion of the same trials that all other boys had had to pass from time immemorial) there would be no "proof" that the child had changed form – from boy to man. Other examples of well-known transformation include the conquests of vast lands by Rome that transformed a city into an Empire; the fall of the Holy Roman Empire that transformed the world into what we now refer to as the Dark Ages, the transformation of South Africa from Apartheid to equality, or the transformation of a star into a black hole.

In other words, changes profound enough to be called a transformation are not routine, "it happened one sunny morning," sorts of changes. We may decide to make significant and difficult changes in our lives because we know it would be better for us. But we do not just decide to transform ourselves from one form into another[51] – something compelling propels us into such changes – often kicking and screaming we are dragged into the journey. In the process we are transformed.

One of the most often cited instances of personal transformation is the near-death experience. A successful businessman who spent months at death's door as a result of a grim boating accident returned to his ordinary life, resigned his CEO post and became a father active in his children's lives. He went back to school and got a fine arts degree. The story is told of St. Francis of Assisi that it was in recovering from the injuries inflicted in a brawl that he changed the course of his life from being heir to his father's business to the saint we know today. Transformation of this sort is hardly a rational decision, one that a person would make some bright Monday morning.

Businesses transform because they can no longer do business in the old way. One of the problems American military leaders struggle with is the very success of the military. They know that the world is changing. They know that warfare is changing. They know that they need an integrated digital environment and that requires a culture change. And the military has made significant changes. It has not transformed – it's been too successful and significantly rewarded monetarily for that success.

Transformation as process

What we are transforming into is a new age – one we can only begin to imagine. The process we and others are going through is not new – it is as old as the earliest fairy tales. It is as profound as the stories we learned on our parent's knee – or sneaking away to the library to read on our own. It is a transformation that scares the wits out of us – just like the stories and myths that are part of our very being.

This culture transformation is one that promises to change profoundly not only the work culture, but the culture at large, as well. A deeper understanding of this journey will help us master for ourselves and lead others through the transformation. Knowledge will protect us from being buffeted about by the transformation as victims of a little-understood process. We will know, and understand, what is happening to us. That does not make the transformation any less painful – or any less terrifying, but it does help us navigate the shoals of change.

---

[51] The enchanted frog does not just decide to become a prince. He must wait until some princess will kiss him. Such an event only happens when the princess' world has been threatened in some significant way. No self-respecting princess just decides to kiss a frog.

We use the language of the hero's journey to outline the challenges, the mileposts, and the signs along the way in the work of culture transformation.

A language that makes sense of transformation

We have said that transformation is a very special kind of change – a profound and fundamental change in the way things are. The vocabulary of myth is an older, more universal and multi-layered language better adapted to speaking of such things by giving us mental pictures, memorable stories, and symbols that stay with us.

As we noted in earlier chapters, Campbell and Jung gave us the rich palette of colors for painting a picture of transformation by reminding us that heroes are ordinary people – people just like those who live today – when they begin their journey. They are called out of their old way, a way that has become too confining to nurture them. They stumble through unknown territory; are forced to meet obstacles and endure trials that seem unconquerable; find help in unexpected places and emerge with a "boon," a new (transformed) way of seeing, being, doing. They experience life and reality differently when they return from their adventures. If we hope to understand how to transform – ourselves or our work culture – there is much to learn from the stories, pictures, and symbols of transformation described in myth and tales.

In this century Rosamund and Ben Zander[52] add their own voices and argue that the history of transformational phenomena like the Internet and paradigm shifts in science suggest that transformation does not happen by arguing cogently for something new. They define transformation as a shift in a culture's "experience of the basis for reality."[53]

In other words, transformation is not a rational process – we don't transform by making cogent arguments about the need for change – to others or to ourselves. We must experience reality differently.

Psychologists understand heroes as representations of aspects of the psychological stages each of us passes through on the way to maturity; moving from immaturity to maturity is a process of transformation. Myths

---

[52] Rosamund Zander is an executive coach, a family systems therapist and business consultant, who believes that creativity is essential to healthy adult development. Ben Zander conducts the Boston Philharmonic and has since its inception in 1979. He is also a highly regarded motivational speaker.
[53] Zander, Rosamund & Benjamin. The Art of Possibility. Boston: Harvard Business School Press, 2000, p.4.

and tales give us a way to conceptualize the transforming journey through life.[54] They instruct us in how to meet the fears, pitfalls, duties and requirements of life successfully – that is why they all end happily. (Who, after all, needs instruction on how to screw it up and end up unhappy? We can do that just fine on our own, thank you very much.)

Throughout history the tales we've told each other as a culture (myths, folk tales and fairy tales) have used rich symbolism and metaphor to tell about the transforming journeys we travel as a people – much as dreams do for the individual. Myths and fairy tales tell a people what pitfalls and challenges to expect along the way. They instruct on how to react in difficult situations. In short, they collect the wisdom of a culture and teach a people what to do in order to survive each transforming experience – "to live happily ever after."

The trick, of course, is to decode their shrouded symbols.

In myth and tale, patterns emerge that tell us what to expect and how heroes react so that they come out at the end living happily ever after, as masters of their realm. In the transformation from the ordinary everyday self into the master of the realm, there are certain recognizable stages present in almost all myths and tales.

The transformation into the Knowledge Age is upon us – driven by dramatic and far-reaching technologies that intrude on our lives and our ways of working. The question is not so much whether we will change, but how we will change and how we will feel about it – whether it is a healthy transformation or one racked with strife and heartache. Those of us who want to midwife the Knowledge Age into being will take the same Hero's Journey of transformation as so many others have done in previous times of transformation. Bringing the Knowledge Age into being requires nothing less than a transformation of the culture of work.

Work Culture Transformation

In my recent work with a work culture transformation group, I heard it lamented again and again, by intelligent, capable, powerful leaders that the work culture was "in the way" of making the changes needed. If we

---

[54] For example: In the process of growing up little girls often "get off the straight and narrow" path prescribed by their mothers, as does Little Red Riding Hood. They meet the world's "wolves," pick the much more interesting flowers offered just off the prescribed path, and suffer the consequences. If all goes right, the happy ending is reached if the father comes to her rescue. In this process she is transformed from a little girl to a mature one.

are ever to see the actualization of the promises of workplace improvement touted by technologists, the work culture itself must change profoundly. But how? This seems to be a question that stymies many organizations. It is a question that evokes partial answers: leadership training, pursuit of excellence, total quality management, change management, business process reengineering. These approaches bring about valuable change, but they do not transform the workplace. Technology changes, but the work culture all too often remains the same. The technology is not the promised boon. Technology is one enabler of the promised boon. The boon is the transformed work culture that supports the creation of knowledge, facilitated by technology.

Small changes, as Russia's czar found out in 1917, can't bring about the transformation that will bring the culture into the new century. French kings who tried reform found that evolutionary changes did not fulfill the longings of people to participate in their community life. Reform efforts of the English in their colonies – east and west, south and north – likewise did little to quell the democratic stirrings that eventually formed new nations, new cultures. When the revolution in each of these places was over, the cultures left in place were changed in fundamental ways – they were transformed.

The point is that transformation takes something on the magnitude of a revolution to jolt us from one culture (the habits, traditions, common sense, beliefs, and all the things we **know** about how the world works) to another. That's why transformation is rare in our personal lives, why it is so hard for successfully operating companies and organizations to undertake in the stride of their daily, well-oiled lives. That's why we don't transform our political institutions, why the church, or education, or the military doesn't change in fundamental culture.

When we've painted ourselves into a corner; when we have hit our nadir; when nothing is working any more; as a last resort, we transform – we change form in profound, essential, fundamental ways. Often, life gives us no choice in the matter. Our freedom of choice is overtaken by events.

We do seem to be perverse creatures, don't we? Our saving grace seems to be that we each have different boiling points. What is intolerable to one may be endured for an interminable time by another. One person trapped in a corner of a freshly painted room sees an opportunity for making interesting footprint designs around the perimeter or across the middle. One person's nadir is another's plateau. One marriage partner declares "nothing's working here; I quit," the other responds, "huh, what do you mean? I thought things were just fine."

Better equipped

By understanding the hero's journey, both leaders and those caught up in the transformation as workers will be better equipped to see, manage, and lead this transformation. And they will experience the changes in different ways.

For both groups, being forewarned is being forearmed. Leaders who make decisions about the form that the transformations will take may feel more in control. Workers who are invited on the journey as collaborators will likewise know what to expect, not be taken by surprise and, therefore, feel more in control. Leaders and workers who do not understand the transformation process nor are empowered to participate in it will kick and scream all the louder. Ignorance of what to expect of the process and the ignominy of disempowerment will fuel frustration and anger.

Myths give us a language with which to understand the transformation process, whether it takes place in our individual lives or in the life of an organization. Understanding this language will leave us better equipped for the journey of transformation.

CHAPTER 5

Four Stages of Transformation

In which we attempt to organize the messy business of transformation into four manageable stages.

Now we turn our attention to the discussion of the four stages a hero goes through – the stages identified and articulated by Campbell. Understanding these stages will help us understand the Tale of Rumpelstiltskin. . . . about the man who turns straw into gold.

Four Stages of Transformation

1 The call to adventure, in which life deals a disorienting blow
2 Wandering in the wilderness, in which the hero meets the monsters
3 Help from unexpected places, which makes successful monster-fighting possible
4 Returning with the boon, in which a renewed hero brings good to the culture

> ### The Busy-Mind, One-Word version
>
> 1 Call
> 2 Wandering
> 3 Aid
> 4 Triumph

These four, universal, steps provide the basis for us to understand transformation in general and the transformation of the workplace in particular.

Transformation, personal or organizational, is not a straightforward process, nor is it a controlled process. It comes about because the environment in which we live changes – in a dramatic manner. It is precipitated by an event – and is propelled by forces greater than any one of us.

We are cast out into a new world without signs or guideposts.

Those who rescue us are not under our control either – they come from unexpected places.

The triumph that emerges in the transformation process is not, therefore, a planned process that can be controlled and manipulated.

Being open to transformation is necessary in order for us to triumph – to be willing to accept (if not like) the various two-by-fours that come our way. They are precipitants of transformation, if we will but see them in that light. We will still duck, but enough of them will hit home and set transformation processes underway.

Stage I of the Hero's Journey: The Call

In ancient times the tales of transformation usually began with the unwitting protagonist being hit over the head by the cosmic two-by-four of some highly emotionally charged life event. Campbell calls this the "Call to Adventure," the adventure is the hero's journey. Receiving a call sounds very civilized, like fun, even, since it is a call to adventure. But Campbell then goes on to describe the manners in which this call can be issued. The call to adventure is not a polite call at the door in the Victorian fashion, not a nice tap on the shoulder, not even the midnight phone call. It is not what Christians consider "the call" to serve God or the Church, not a call into a certain vocation, or "calling." Campbell uses it in a myth-specific way.

> *But whether small or great, and no matter what the stage or grade of life, the call rings up the curtain, always, on a mystery of transfiguration – a rite, or moment, of spiritual passage...*[55]

This mystery of transformation is tantamount to dying to the old and being re-born into a new life. The old familiar life has been outgrown;

---
[55] Campbell, Hero with a Thousand Faces, p. 51.

old ideas, ideals, concepts, beliefs and emotional patterns are not adequate to describe or live life. Something just doesn't fit. It is time to cross a threshold. When this mis-fit gets too uncomfortable, life offers a call to transform.

The call comes in a variety of ways:

By blunder

Sometimes the call to adventure is issued by what seems to be a blunder; we blunder into an unsuspected world, as did the Princess who lost the golden ball to a deep pool.[56]

By death

Sometimes the call to adventure is issued by a death that changes the circumstances of the hero's life. The death of a parent or beloved uncle or grandmother may externalize the death of an old pattern of dependence. Cinderella's[57] call comes in this way. Her mother dies, catapulting Cinderella into a family of evil stepsisters who transform her from beloved daughter to a cinder maid.

By loss

One can be called to transform when a significant relationship is lost: Psyche[58] begins her adventure bereft when she loses her adored husband Eros (Cupid) as a result of breaking her promise not to look on his face.

By duping

The call may be issued by a "charlatan" like the one that duped Jack[59] into trading his family's last resource for a pack of beans – which got him summarily sent to bed without any supper by an irate and desperate widowed mother. His adventure began when he saw and climbed the unnatural stalk growing outside his window.

---

[56] This is a tale of transformation from childhood into adolescence, which in primitive cultures is marked with the solemnity of a rite of passage, where the initiate clearly passes through a literal threshold, thereby passing through the symbolic one of entering a new phase in life. See the Frog King, retold in the appendix.
[57] Cinderella and all of the tales to which the author alludes are retold, alphabetically, in Appendix I.
[58] Psyche and Eros is retold in Appendix I.
[59] Jack and the Beanstalk is retold in Appendix I.

In all of the fairy tales and myths the heroes were called out of their ordinary lives in messy ways. The Call to Adventure when issued to the modern hero is no less messy and life-disrupting than that depicted in myth. For example:

Nelson Mandela, the transformer of modern South Africa, launched his journey to leadership of a newly liberated country many years before when he set himself in opposition to the status quo and suffered through a harsh prison sentence.

Eli Wiesel began his journey through the unfathomable hardship of a concentration camp. His powerful writing continues to transform others today.

Each of these heroes encountered a significant emotional event, a blow that left each reeling, ungrounded from the usual routine, about to enter a strange realm, about to open a new chapter of life.

Summarizing Stage I

Heroes of ancient myth and tale, like those of today, are jerked from their normal routines by some cataclysmic event.

Next we turn our attention to their wandering through a wilderness, a dense forest, an unknown land devoid of any of the familiar trappings – no signposts, no landmarks to guide the journey – none of the old rules apply. When Joseph Campbell introduces the idea of the wilderness, he describes it this way:

> *Beyond them (the heroes) is darkness, the unknown, and danger; just as beyond the parental watch is danger to the infant and beyond the protection of his society danger to the member of the tribe.*[60]

Stage II of the Hero's Journey: Wandering

What better reason is there for refusing (or trying to refuse) the call than knowing that you must enter the wilderness, the darkness, face the abyss, sail off the edge of the known world? Columbus had to threaten, cajole, and urge on his men as they entered the territory that the well-known maps of the medieval world marked "here be monsters." Through another well-known wilderness, Moses, like Columbus, had to prod along the "children" of Israel with promises of a land of milk and honey. By

---

[60] Campbell. Hero with a Thousand Faces. P. 77–78.

doing so he urged them along their journey of 40 years in the wilderness – where they met hardship and deprivation, were tempted to make other gods, like the ones that protected the known world they had left behind, and for whose safety they longed.[61]

Ulysses on his odyssey meets a monster with one eye. What rules govern making one's way through a cyclops-ruled land? Snow White goes to the deep woods and lives with dwarves. What in the world do you do to make your way in a dwarf-infested forest primeval? Where is Emily Post when Beauty must dine nightly with the Beast? Where is the instruction book for spinning a mountain of straw to gold and gaining exodus from the locked room and a certain death penalty?

The Lapp shamans, while in deep trance, journey across high mountains, cross arid deserts, and traverse dense forests. Often on this journey they find the bones of other shamans who have not successfully met the perils of the wilderness. Shamans and medicine men of primitive societies take on the journey for others who have been hit by the cosmic two-by-four and effect their transformation for them. In our society, in the words of the old spiritual, "Nobody else can do it for you, you gotta climb that mountain for yourself." Lacking a shaman, therefore, if you would effect a transformation, you must answer the call yourself, and set forth into the wild unknown.

For Mary Catherine Bateson, daughter of Margaret Mead and Gregory Bateson, at a peak in her career, an accumulation of emotional events sent her "wandering" this way:

> *My mother died in 1978; within two months, I had lost a job and a home to the Iranian revolution. It took a year to deal with the complexities of closing my mother's office; then in 1980, just before I began a new job, my father died.*[62]

At a very difficult point in an extraordinary life, Alfred I. Du Pont wrote of his wilderness experience. To an old friend, he wrote that he was:

> *. . . .arranging to take a little vacation in the West. . . , and once I get away from my secretary, I doubt if anyone will ever hear from me. . . . .I find I am badly in need of a little nervous rest.*[63]

---

[61] How often do we, when threatened, try to return to the safety of the good old days? In those days rules were rules, there was a black and a white, good and evil were clearly defined – at least that's the way we remember them, or some would say romanticize them.

[62] Bateson, M. K. Composing a Life. New York: Penguin, 1990, p. 221.

[63] Wall, Joseph Frazier. Alfred I. Du Pont: The man and his family. New York: Oxford University Press, 1990, p.421.

58 *Universal Stages of Transformation*

To his fiancee, of the same period, he wrote:

> *I can't see a map ahead at this time. My business affairs in New York are in an awful mess & the trip to California & back had only added to the mess & I don't think there is any solution save a liquidation...* [64]

When the hero begins the journey, in myth, tale, or modern life, all feels lost. Old rules don't apply; there is no road map. There is no consultant to hire, no software that can organize the chaos. Furthermore, colleagues may deride as idealistic, romantic, or just plain crazy the idea of leaving the tried and true, the known way. "Why risk it?" "What if you make the wrong decision?" or "How do you know this is going to work?" come the taunts of what Campbell called the "usual people" (i.e. non-heroes). These people would refuse the call, remain within the described bounds. They may even build a Minos Empire[65] – a vast labyrinth that seeks to hide one from one's monster. Many watch closely, waiting for the hero to make a fatal mistake, proving their conservatism right.

Summarizing Stage II

The horror of getting lost in this yawning abyss, this monster-laden swamp, this no-man's land is so great that many a could-be hero declines the challenge of the journey at this point and retreats – or gives up and moves away. It takes a hero's courage to face the abandonment of friends who not only refuse the journey, but belittle the hero for the lack of wisdom shown in a willingness to leave the tried and true, the known, the proven. The dejection, the depression, the hopelessness is hard to bear and the learning curve is steep when all the known landmarks which could accelerate the learning are absent. Indeed, it takes a hero to proceed through this threshold.

For those who persevere, hope is on the way.

---

[64] Ibid., p. 423.
[65] King Minos, himself a product of his mother, Europa's mating with Zeus in the form of a bull, responded to the birth of a monster (result of his wife's mating with a bull) by building a labyrinth. This labyrinth was an effort to contain the flesh-eating monster/son. Athens had to dedicate a tribute of seven youths and seven maidens each year until Theseus slew the Minotaur.

Stage III of the Hero's Journey: Help from unlikely places

A hero thrown into the abyss is not abandoned by the gods.

Someone or something is sent to help the dejected hero.

The cruel joke, though, is that the help is usually in the form of something the hero would usually overlook, disdain or reject – or someone the hero considers distasteful, disgusting, or threatening.

When the protagonist is at the lowest point (nothing seems to be working, all the usual mental functions or coping mechanisms are broken – in short, the hero is in the wilderness) aid comes. And from where? In myths and tales it is often from birds, a fish, the bees, an old hag, an aged hermit, a befriending monster. In short, help comes from some unusual, often little known or respected place.

After Jack has climbed the Beanstalk, the Giant's wife helps him hide in a churn. A frog helps the princess retrieve her gold ball from the well. The ants sort Psyche's impossible mountain of millet, poppy seed, and wheat – a task imposed by Aphrodite, the vengeful mother of Eros. Rumpelstiltskin, a repugnant gnome, walks through the locked door and sits down to spin the straw into gold.

From where does the modern hero's help come at the nadir? (If we could answer that question with a precise, helpful answer, help would hardly be coming from an unexpected place.) We should expect help, but we don't know from where – "if only we had a crystal ball, a map, or even a friend," we plead.

It might come from a brilliant insight that arrives like a bolt of lightning while talking to a friend; it might come from daydreaming, or night dreaming. Creativity, inspiration and insight are often called "gifts" because they cannot be predicted or planned or ordered. But they are the very unexpected gift of which knowledge is made. Help in the wilderness will not come from any of the usual books, websites, professional consultations – if it does, it's not the sort of help about which the tales of the hero's journey speak.

The help may come from without, from some "dwarf" that is a figure of derision: an enemy at work, a despised boss or colleague, someone whose whole job description to date has been to make the hero's life miserable. This sort of help from outside is reminiscent of the Zen admonition that everyone is our teacher, particularly those to whom we have extremely negative reactions – if we can but learn the lesson.

Elias Howe found the solution to making a machine that would sew from a nightmare[66] – that un-respected "Rumpelstilskin" from the

---

[66] Taylor, Jeremy. Dream Work: Techniques for Discovering the Creative Power in Dreams. New York: Paulist Press. 1983, p.7.

60 *Universal Stages of Transformation*

unconscious not usually seen as a source of help. His 1844 discovery transformed the hand-labor of making clothes into an industry. The machine took over the productive process. The thread was already spun by mechanical "spinning jennies" and made into cloth by machine-driven looms – the transformation of the industry awaited only Howe's sewing machine.

During a painful "wilderness" time in her life, a Brazilian anthropologist took Johnnetta Cole, then a professor at Hunter College, to meet Maruca, a diviner in Sao Paulo. What more unexpected place than a Yoruba diviner for re-framing this period in her life and holding out hope for change for this educated, respected, college professor? When she describes the visit, she tells of arriving at a working-class neighborhood and being conducted into the diviner's bedroom where cowrie shells, water, a snake plant, and carved images that kept away the evil eye were assembled. The diviner looked at Dr. Cole with her soul-penetrating eyes and then acted as a medium rather than a diviner.

> *She looked at me and said 'You are about to change your job, to do something that is very close to what you now do but it's different and it's what very few women do in your country.*[67]

The Yoruba diviner told her that it was a very important job and that the island gods could guide her.

Dr. Cole dismissed the help, thinking "I'm not even looking for a job – and I certainly don't believe in divination."[68]

If help when all seems lost can be found in nightmares or through a Yoruba diviner, it would be unwise of a modern hero to scorn help offered from the most unlikely of sources. The psyche in all its perversity seems to choose each hero's "dwarf" to offer the needed help – as if the cosmic joke followed inevitably on the heels of the bonk on the head by the cosmic two-by-four.

Summarizing Stage III

Expect help, but leave yourself open to its arrival through the most unusual channels imaginable – even via an enemy, sorcerer, dream image, or jokester.

---

[67] Bateson, p 30.
[68] patience is begged of the reader; the denouement comes in Stage IV.

Stage IV of the Hero's Journey: Triumph – returning with the boon

Finally the hero comes to the end of the journey. Life's catastrophe was seen as a call to transform. The poor hero took on the map-less journey, accepted the unlikely help and voilà – finds the treasure, is blessed by the gods, gets the gold – now it is time to return triumphant, and bask in the achievements.

This is the mythmakers' way of saying, "if you eat your spinach and say your prayers, you'll go to heaven" – of course, psychologically speaking. In other words, if you meet the psychological challenges that everyone faces in life in the process of maturing, and meet them in specific ways, you will triumph. Each myth or tale addresses one of the challenges faced in growing up, maturing – transforming.

The hero of ancient myth and tale always returns triumphant – to live happily ever after – usually bringing great good to the community in the process. Hansel and Gretel return home with the jewels hoarded in the Gingerbread House; Jason returns with the Golden Fleece; the Cinder maid becomes queen of the realm, and the Miller's daughter becomes wife to the King.

When heroes complete a successful journey their life and the world around them is filled with renewed energy – energy that again flows from hero to world to hero in a self-renewing pattern.

When Johnnetta Cole, who didn't believe the Yoruba diviner, returned to New York in August she found on her desk an invitation from the search committee to become president of Spellman College. In her tenure as President of that institution she found herself mirrored, "feeling natural," using all her faculties and training and knowledge.[69]

Mary Catherine Bateson says that when she finished the chaotic period in her life (a revolution, the death of her parents and the loss of her job) she was finally able to say that she was a writer.[70]

Alfred du Pont's legendary financial success (after believing that his only way out of the financial swamp he was in was to liquidate all) hardly needs to be documented. The same can be said of the heroes whose names have become household words: people like Nelson Mandela and Eli Wiesel. Often unnamed heroes battled through the abyss to bring a boon that changed our world: those who crafted the American Revolution and Constitution, today's astronauts and the scientists who support them,

---

[69] Bateson. p. 226.
[70] Ibid., p. 222

inventors of the machinery that ushered in the Industrial Age – hopefully the diversity of categories alone will stimulate the readers' imagination about heroes.

Summarizing Stage IV

The modern hero will be one who can take on the journey and return with a boon,[71] a blessing, a treasure – the flow of new life and energy into the world. In other words, transformation brings rewards, but you don't start with the rewards and work backward to figure out the steps to get there – the way you might if you were working on a project. You only get to the reward if you heed the cosmic two-by-four that disrupts your life, see it as an opportunity, accept the call and step out of the bounds of your regular life. With the courage to sustain the wandering in the wilderness, to meet and engage the monsters, you put one foot in front of the other in uncertain times and terrifying places, trusting that you will make the journey successfully.

---

[71] One of the most fitting definitions of "boon" given in the Oxford English Dictionary is "a thing freely or graciously given."

CHAPTER 6

Personal and Organizational Transformation

In which we investigate the parallels between personal and organizational transformation

Now that we have the four universal stages for transformation firmly in mind, we can look at them from various angles and better understand the transformation process that we are going through. No matter where we are; no matter what we do; these four stages will be our guide to understanding and feeling the possibility for a new way to do work.

Personal Transformation

The call

In personal life, extreme emotional experiences leave us dazed. Experiences like the death of someone close, the loss of a long and stabilizing marriage, a near-death experience, the loss of a home to a flood or hurricane, succumbing to a financially-wrecking scam, or the refugee experience (naming but a few) can so disrupt life that it leaves us feeling lost, depressed, and uprooted. Such experiences can serve to demoralize and debilitate us; or they can be used as a call to an expanded and redefined life. In choosing the latter response, we have accepted the call to adventure. And accepting the call is only the first step of a long and arduous recovery period.

The wilderness/wandering

Often a personal transformation is experienced first as a deep depression. When a life-changing event throws us into terra incognita, before we can find or make new signposts in this land, we experience the disorientation as depression.

Help/aid

If clients ask a psychotherapist what the outcome of a depression will be, we can promise hope, we outline the process and offer knowledge and support for the journey. But foolish is the therapist who gazes into a crystal ball and predicts the future.

At best one can say, "It depends. . ."

Will you accept the challenge of change as a call to adventure, the invitation to leave the known and enter the unknown?

Are you willing, or have you the strength to encounter dragons, muck through swamps, and scale glacier-covered mountains?

Can you be open to unexpected sources of help – not turn from the hag who demands a kiss or scorn the ant that offers you help to sort the lentils?

The boon/triumph

Once you've slain the dragon and rescued the treasure, will you bring it back to your community to make the world a better place?

If the client can find the "Yes!" to each of the questions, then we can predict recovery. We still cannot say exactly what life will look like in the recovered state. We cannot predict exactly how long it will take to arrive there or how long each stage will last. We can simply say that good will come out of this depression if the client will take the journey.

Organizational transformation

Organizations, just like people, go through these same four stages – the call, the wandering, unexpected help and the boon – as they are caught in the crosswinds of transformation.

Making the kind of cultural transformation that will move us from one age to another is not just a rational decision. Transformation is not easy, not undertaken in the "mood of cold, ironic realism."[72] We need to

---

[72] Brooks, David. "A Man on a Gray Horse," Atlantic Monthly, September 2002.

remember that people need to have their hearts kindled, their hopes fired, and their passions engaged. Firebrands like Patrick Henry and Thomas Paine fueled the American Revolution. Without them we might still be making logical plans for a change from British rule.

Trying to transform the culture at the decision level (the cold, ironic realism mode) complete with a set of road maps and ordered, feasible steps so that the project can be managed reasonably, will not transform the work culture. People must have their hopes fired and their passions engaged. They must experience reality differently. Trying to transform an organization by carefully following a complete road map with feasible steps will fail precisely because it deals only at the decision level – not with the reality of life as it is lived . . . and as it changes.

The call

Today's business hero might be plunged into chaos by the failure of a company, loss of the biggest customer, or theft of significant amounts of money from the till. The catastrophic loss of budget, personnel or equipment, or the introduction of a new technology[73] that changes the fundamental way work is done may be the cosmic two-by-four. It may begin with a career change, the quick and unexpected loss of a job or a business failure.

For many seasoned medical professionals, the drastic change in health care is such call to transform. The old ways of the respected professional with the time to bring the healing touch is being overwhelmed by the demands of a rapidly aging population, new stresses and strains, and health care institutions that cannot meet the needs of patients. In business the call can arrive because of war, depression, acquisition or failure. A natural disaster might trigger a transformation.

The Wilderness

That period of disorientation and disorganization that follows the emotionally laden event that threatens or ends the life of an organization is the business parallel of the personal wilderness.

Any one of these events leads some organizations to decline the call to adventure implied by such an event. In such cases, the organization might cease to exist or limp along into bankruptcy or decline. Or, many organizations try a variety of solutions, many of which work to

---

[73] For example, when diesel fuel replaced coal on steam engines, it meant that thousands of coal-sholveling firemen were out of work, their profession re-defined.

re-organize, re-prioritize, re-envision, or re-engineer the business processes. Such organizations may emerge from such a change revitalized and profitable. They do not emerge transformed from a frog to a prince – with a whole new way to do work.

The chaos of change can serve as a call to transformation. The response to the call cannot be simply trying harder or working smarter or doing better. Answering the call to the hero's journey will result in living life or doing business in a whole new way.

Heroes who are transformed in turn transform their worlds.

The depressed martyr who transforms into a blooming, productive writer is a boon to her children and her readers.

A business that is transformed from a dying relic to a thriving hive of creativity is one where people want to work. It is a boon to its community.

A bitter quadriplegic veteran transformed to an inspiring artist who paints with a brush in his mouth is an inspiration to those around him.

A too-busy businessman who becomes an involved father and partner brings new energy not only to his family but also to those in his world.

It is both possible and "reasonable" to refuse the call

Let's think for a moment of the cosmic two-by-four as an event equivalent to the bewitching of a prince into a frog. The frog cannot simply decide one lovely spring morning that he wants to be a prince again. He can't make a plan and manage the project according to the best practices and following the best road map. There is a lot of wilderness to be crossed, better called a swamp in this case, and impossible tasks to be accomplished. Poor frog must find a princess willing to kiss his ugly face before he can hope to be transformed back into a prince. None of his favorite royal consultants have proven much use – they can't even understand the language he speaks as a frog. He knows the petulant nature of many princesses and therefore may shrink from his task – sinking into the life of the quiet desperation of a frog doomed to catch flies in summer and sleep in the mud in the winter.

Joseph Campbell put it this way:

> *Often in actual life, and not infrequently in the myths and popular tales, we encounter the dull case of the call unanswered; for it is always possible to turn the ear to other interests.*[74]

---

[74] Campbell, Hero with a thousand faces. op. cit., p. 59

Even though it is not necessary that we accept the call to transformation, the decision (or the lack of decision) that causes us to turn our backs on change will often leave us in an even more unhappy state and situation. Accepting the call is scarier – but it is often better than the alternative – being frozen in an outmoded way of living.

Campbell gives examples of mythic figures who refused the call. All of them are "stuck" in lives of boredom, hard work, and an inability to move forward. Refusing the call has dire consequences.

So now, at last we turn ourselves to the magic of making gold from straw – and turn our attention to one of the richest tales of them all: the tale of a little man who did powerful things, a beautiful maiden who managed to survive, and a community who helped her along. We turn to the tale of Rumpelstiltskin.

And we see the four stages of transformation before our eyes.

SECTION IV

From Straw to Gold

In which we re-tell and analyze the tale of Rumpelstiltskin and explain why it was chosen from the infinite pool of fairy tales as the tale that will help us understand Transformation of the Work Culture, the Modern Hero's Journey.

Once upon a time a funny little man named Rumpelstiltskin saved a maiden's life by spinning her heap of straw into gold.

Today we seek the same power to transform the worthless bits of tasks and data that make up our work into gold – something of value and meaning to ourselves and others.

CHAPTER 7

The Tale of Rumpelstiltskin

In which we re-tell an old tale.

Do you remember that once upon a time there was a poor miller who had a beautiful daughter? And that one day, to make himself look important in the eyes of the king, he bragged that his daughter could spin straw into gold? The king, being very enamored of gold, told the miller that he wanted to meet this extraordinarily talented maiden.

When the daughter had been brought to the castle, the king led her to a room filled with straw. He gave her a spinning wheel and spindle and said "If you don't spin this straw into gold by the morning, then you must die." He then locked the door. The maiden, furious at her father for bragging, began slowly to grasp her situation [one which most of us have faced at one time or another]. She was alone in a room full of straw that by morning must be gold – an impossible task with an impossible deadline. She quickly moved through the various stages of mourning. Her fear and despair grew. She began to weep.

Suddenly the door opened and a little man entered and said simply, "Good evening, Mistress Miller. Why are you weeping so?" [The transformation was about to begin. She had been hit by the cosmic two-by-four – crossed the threshold. Her wilderness was a dungeon, no comforts of home there.]

"I have to spin this straw into gold, and I don't know how."

The little man asked, "What will you give me if I spin it for you? I know how to do it."

"My necklace, I'll give you my necklace," the maiden replied.

The little man [we would call him a "guru" consultant, but decided against this after looking at the relatively tepid success that many gurus have] took the necklace, put it in his pocket and sat down to the task.

Whizz, whizz, whizz: He filled one spool after the other with fine gold thread. When morning came, the room was filled with spools of gold instead of mountains of straw.

The king appeared at sunrise. When he saw all the gold he was surprised and pleased, but, [like many managers and entrepreneurs,] his heart grew ever more greedy. For two more days, he repeated his threat and his instructions to turn the straw into gold. Each night the maiden wept; each night the door opened and the little man appeared asking "And what will you give me if I spin this room full of straw into gold?" Each night the price went up until the maiden had nothing left to give except the promise of her firstborn child. [The price of success was getting a bit steep.]

When the king returned on the third day, he said, "This time, if you succeed, you shall become my wife."

The king was so delighted with the third room of gold he married the beautiful (and quite talented) miller's daughter.[75]

Time went by.

After a year the queen gave birth to a beautiful child. The funny little man appeared – as promised – and demanded the final payment for his gold-spinning services.

The horrified queen offered him all the treasures of the kingdom if he would just let her keep her child. The little man was adamant, "Something living is more important to me than all the treasures in the world."

[Rumpelstiltskin knew his values ... and they were not bad ones.]

---

[75] This is one happy ending, the tale could end here having addressed one psychological challenge. This tale, however, continues to a "what they did after the marriage chapter."

The beautiful queen began to grieve and weep so much that the little man felt sorry for her, for he had a heart – and not just valuable knowledge. "I'll give you three days' time," he said. "If you can guess my name by the third day, you shall keep your child."

The first night the queen recalled every name she had ever heard. She also realized that she needed some help, so she sent her servants and friends out into the countryside to collect names. On the following day when the little man appeared, she began to recite all the names, "Kaspar, Melchior, Balzer . . ." After each one the little man said, "That's not my name."

The second day she sent out even more messengers to scour the countryside for every obscure name they could find. When the little man appeared the second day, she went through all the unusual names she had found. "Is it Ribsofbeef? Or Muttonchops? Or Lacedleg?" But each time he replied, "That's not my name."

The little man left feeling smug – his possession of the child all but assured.

The beautiful queen desperately sent out her messengers yet again. Toward the end of the third day, a messenger – a real friend – returned and reported that he couldn't find a single new name. "But high in a mountain at the edge of the forest, where the fox and the hare say goodnight to each other," he said, "I saw a small cottage, and in front of the cottage was a fire, and around the fire danced a ridiculous little man. He was hopping on one leg and screeching:

'Today I'll brew, tomorrow I'll bake.
Soon I'll have the queen's namesake.
Oh, how hard it is to play my game
For Rumpelstiltskin is my name!'"

The queen was beside herself with joy. As soon as the little man entered and asked, "What's my name, Your Highness?" she teased him with her first two answers.

"Is your name Kunz?"
"No," chortled the little man
"Is it Heinz?"
"Nope," he danced.
"Could it be Rumpelstiltskin?"

"The devil told you! The devil told you!" the little man screamed [not knowing the power of friends and co-workers in a time of need]. He stamped so ferociously with his right foot that his leg went deep into the ground up to his waist. Then he grabbed the other foot angrily with both hands and ripped himself in two.

So ended the life of that spinner of gold.[76]

---

[76] After the translation of Jack Zipes as found in *The Complete Fairy Tales of the Brothers Grimm*. New York: Bantam. 1987.

CHAPTER 8

Why Rumpelstiltskin?

In which we attempt to justify our choice of this tale from the universe of possible choices.

We could take almost any fairy tale or myth and gain insight into how transformation is accomplished, if we can use not the literal part of our brains, but the part that sees "between the lines."[77] Rumpelstiltskin, however, seems particularly apt for the following reasons:

1. This tale is "complete." It has all four stages the hero traverses. An organization or a person in transformation goes through all, generally.
2. The task of spinning straw and producing gold is a clear and overt change of form – a transformation.
3. Producing something of value (gold) is what people want to do in their work.
4. When people find they have exchanged their irreplaceable life's time for "straw," they feel cheated.
5. The metaphor of transformation from lowly chattel to Queen seems appropriate to picture what happens when workers take on work that has value: they are transformed from lowly "daughters" to powerful "Queens." (Men will have to bear with the juggling of the gender problem, I'm afraid.)

---

[77] For more explanation of why it is important to approach the tale with the whole brain, see "seeing with the third eye" in Section V. The literal, fact-oriented part of the brain will want to argue with each point. For a moment, suspend disbelief and know that tales and myths deal with one psychological issue per tale, generally; they do not address the whole complexity of life in one fell swoop.

6 To succeed, the Queen had to collaborate with the community, they had to be united in vision and mission; they had to work as a team (co-labor together) – all hallmarks of a community of practice.
7 The symbol of the King and Queen's baby, the next ruler of the realm, is also a fine symbol for a work culture transformation. With a new ruler come new mores, new expectations, new fashion, in some cases, even new belief systems[78] – in short, new cultures.

Rumpelstiltskin is a tale about transformation. It also serves as a cautionary tale about the consequences of hoarding information and working without the benefit of community. It provides us a new way to think about (among other things) the profound changes taking place as we adapt the way we do work and the way we think about work to the realities of the technical advances of the late twentieth century.

The act of transformation involved when the wee gnome, Rumpelstiltskin, changes an everyday worthless substance to something of value seems to describe what each of us wants from our work. We go to work wanting to provide something of value (gold). We are often derailed in our attempt to accomplish this noble task by the work culture in which we attempt to make gold. The work culture often deals us a mountain of meaningless tedium and insurmountable problems (straw). We are all struggling with how to face the straw of our work and transform it to gold, the ideal that brought us to work in the first place.

Rumpelstiltskin in the Cheat-Sheet, Nutshell form

A maiden's father overstates her abilities to the King. The King calls the father's bluff and tests the daughter to see if the father has told the truth. He has not, but nonetheless she is locked into a dungeon, given her old tool for spinning but asked to produce gold, not thread. She despairs. A knowledgeable stranger appears and produces the new product, but ups the ante with each visit and leaves behind no instruction for the maiden to reproduce his results.[79] The final price demands that the

---

[78] Conversion en masse to Christianity of the Rus when Prince Vladimir became leader, and the slow replacement of local tribal allegiance when the El Saud came to power in Arabia are two examples that come to mind.

[79] Many readers, clients and trainees argue that the maiden *should* have tried other ways to achieve her means. We'll not go into rewriting fairy tales, though, that, too, is an interesting activity. We'll deal here with what the maiden did and the way the tale came to us from the middle ages. Her actions led to particular results that taught particular lessons.

maiden, soon-to-be Queen, give up the heir to the kingdom in payment. The Queen rebels when the time comes to make the final payment and the stranger appears to relent, but secretly knows he will win the prize because he has set an impossible task. The Queen calls together the community that meets his demands, destroying him. The community brings about a culture not ruled by a magic-maker with possession of the secret of making gold from straw, but ruled by a grateful King and Queen who raise a baby destined to bring a new culture.

Rumpelstiltskin in the business form

The manager or sales staff [father] overstates the case for the worker's [maiden's] productive abilities to the leadership or customers [king]. The leader or customer calls the manager/sales-staff's bluff and puts the workers to the test. The workers despair, know they can't produce what is asked; not, at least, by any of the old ways they know. In the night, one of those three-o'clock-in-the-morning brilliant flashes comes right up out of the unconscious to the rescue – they get themselves a guru/consultant [Rumpelstiltskin] who could solve the problem.[80] Each time, however, this guru-rescue becomes more expensive and the consultant leaves behind no reports, no instructions, no training, only a higher and higher bill.

The leader rewards the worker(s) with power and position. The manager is off the hook; the workers not only keep their lives (jobs), but also are made co-leaders.

When the consultant returns to try to take away the new generation, the baby, the leader-in-training, the co-leader (Queen) marshals the community of practice [the village], shares the mission with them, empowers them to find/make the knowledge that will save the company (kingdom). They rise to the task, and save the day. They produce the next leader, rather than producing gold – much like teaching a man to fish rather than giving him a fish.

One way of looking at the image of Rumpelstilskin's self-destruction is that the paradigm shifted from knowledge-hoarding being the path to power to communities of practice[81] being the path to power. In Rumpel's paradigm consultants have an expertise that works to make them masters of their field, but they are so busy spinning gold they don't stay connected

---

[80] Reminiscent of Howe's invention of the sewing machine, Fulton's solution to the steam engine, and Stevenson's writing of Treasure Island – each of them wrote from dream inspirations.
[81] A group of people with a common mission. See Appendix 11 for more.

– Rumpel's a hermit, after all – and fail to notice that the world and its technology are changing. COBAL programmers are a recent example – at one time their knowledge was limited to the few and could demand a high price, but they "self-destruct" (become obsolete) when the world around them changes.

So no matter how we approach the tale . . . as a child or as a business person we can feel and understand the truth of transformation. It is not easy – and it goes through the four stages of getting the call and accepting it. It continues through the hero's despair in the locked room, trying to figure out how to do what seems to be impossible, getting help from unexpected places and then returning to life with a new and better understanding, ready to look for the next adventure.

CHAPTER 9

Understanding the Tale

In which we hope to make an ancient tale relevant to modern readers.

As we seek to make sense in modern terms of this medieval tale, there are some things to remember:

(1) Each character in a fairy tale, folk tale, or myth is easily recognized as someone we know from real life. Everyone knows a braggart (like the father in the Rumpelstiltskin tale), a person who has it all yet is still greedy (like the king). We all know a hapless maiden who falls victim to some nefarious scheme; we all know someone who will offer to help, "for a price." These characters are referred to as the external characters; those we recognize from the external world.

(2) The tale itself embodies psychological truth in symbolic fashion; therefore, the characters are also symbolic as parts of our psyches. Tales tell us about psychological phases all people go through in life; they instruct us on how to navigate the difficulties, and warn us of challenges we will face. For example, from time to time each of us is appalled to have made ourselves important in someone else's eyes – perhaps by bragging, lying, or belittling another. Who hasn't been faced with an impossible task with an impossible deadline? And who can claim never to have been greedy or never to have found an answer from a very unlikely, even unbelievable internal or external source? Each of us has had the experience of having a threatening or much feared thing disappear once we can give it a name. In short, not only do the King, Maiden, and Rumpelstiltskin live in our external world; they are alive and well within us in our psyches, too. These will be referred to in the text as internal characters or symbols.

The symbols in the tale and in modern life

The story, of course, is much richer than the cheat-sheet nutshell forms in the front of this chapter and has far more implications. That's the nice thing about symbols, you can talk around them all day and never pin them down to one straight-line, true-for-all-time meaning. The shades of meaning are hues on the artist's palette. You never come to the bottom of their well of meaning.

The characters are symbols that have implications for the personal psyche of the reader; no matter which characters in the tale the reader identifies with at any given time. To plumb some of that richness, we will go through the tale, character by character; symbol by symbol, for the subtleties of their messages. Those with no patience for shades of gray or complexity that will not sort itself out into a neat, straight line, might want to skip this part.

Myths and tales, like the transformation process itself, will simply not just line up and file in, single file. You can't make a 3-step process of transformation:

- not of the transforming process of birth,
- not of the water molecules as they disorganize from water to become steam,
- not of the revolution,
- not of the change from boyhood to manhood,
- not for emerging from a depression that has left you "hanging on the meat hook[82]."

Even though those who eventually leave the "underworld" of depression, like Inanna, and return with a gift from this world that makes their world better – i.e., the transformation experts – can't make a retrospective road map. They could make a map, of sorts, of their journey, but this map would not be one that others could necessarily follow.

Nor will there be a road map to work culture transformation.

As we take the characters, in more-or-less order of appearance, we will discuss the symbol as it appears in the fairy tale. We will also discuss what some of the personal implications might be if we were to use this tale as a mini-tour guide of a particular stage of psychological development. We will also update the symbol, illustrating it and bringing it into modern life.

---

[82] For a synopsis of Inanna, to which this alludes, see Appendix I.

But before we do that, let's satisfy those who just want the bottom line, and go straight to the lesson we draw from the tale.

The lesson

Those of us who peek at the end of a murder mystery to see who-done-it, bottom-liners who just want the facts, ma'am,[83] can get them in this short chapter – no need to be led through the argument of why we reached this conclusion.

Literalists with a mind for detail and facts can say, rightly, that straw is transformed into gold by a dwarf.

Psychologists can say that the trash of our lives is transformed into something of value through the agency of a small, ugly, unvalued part of ourselves.

Workers can say that the unsatisfying parts of their work have been transformed into the satisfaction they seek because their community banded together to find the secret of a new way to do work.

Business leaders can say that the nature of work is transformed from the industrial model to one supporting the Knowledge Age. A new method of spinning (working) replaces the old (the method the maiden would have used to spin thread). And new results accrue – gold is amassed.

Business leaders can further see that a transformation takes place when the community bands together in a common mission and discovers (makes) knowledge (the knowledge of the name of Rumpelstiltskin). Rumpelstiltskin ceases to exist when his name is learned – he has no more power over the kingdom.

What is transformed in the tale of Rumpelstiltskin depends on one's point of view – and they are all correct.

The Maiden (worker) is transformed into Queen, a person with power over her own life.

The work (spinning) is transformed; new ways are introduced, by a despicable character.

The community is the agent of transformation, sent out by the leaders to discover knowledge. In doing so, it ushers in a new regime. The baby they save will one day grow up to be King. Kingdoms with new kings offer the possibility of new rules, new mores and, often, new beliefs, in short, new cultures.

---

[83] Many readers may not remember the character, Detective Joe Friday of the American TV series "Dragnet." He was famous for his investigatory approach that asked for, "the facts, ma'am, just the facts."

Fairy tales were committed to writing at about the time of the Industrial Revolution and often embodied the longings of people for simpler, earlier times – "the good old days." As such, Rumpel is a lovely example of the community's fantasy about a boss who was asking more than they could give.

Today's "King" is the old way of doing business, the Industrial culture that hasn't died yet. The dwarf represents those attitudes and beliefs in us and in our culture (the old artifacts, rules, beliefs and customs) that help us adapt to the unreasonable demands (when applied to the Knowledge Age) of the industrial way of doing business. The king says spin this mess and make me gold, or you die. The dwarf helps us do it. In the end, we rebel, by calling together the community to extricate ourselves from the demands of the dwarf. The community saves the day by finding the name of the dwarf. In ancient cultures a name was a very powerful, magical thing. To know someone's name was to take his or her power. The power of Rumpel was to make gold. His power gone, he died. The tale does not go into the "next chapter;" the chapter that would tell us about what the community did once they had Rumpel's power.

The community finds knowledge, the Knowledge Age's "gold."

People work because they hope to make a difference; work is the quintessential human activity.[84] Having meaningful work is, for many, a greater motivater than money, title or power. When faced with "straw" we, like the miller's daughter, give up hope. We, like she, feel betrayed. When a Rumpelstiltskin comes along, we can see the light of another day. But when the community supports us, we take the power once held in secret and make our own gold. And today's gold is knowledge.

If we look at the overall pattern in the tale of Rumpelstiltskin, we see that it follows the pattern of all Hero's Journeys[85]. The Maiden is faced with a significant emotional event, she is locked into a dungeon, told to perform a miracle, or lose her life. She despairs – her wilderness experience, giving up all hope, none of the old rules apply. Help appears in the form of a dwarf – a highly suspect form of help for the task of spinning straw to gold. (In the era in which the tale was written, dwarves were outcasts from society.) The boon comes in two stages: 1) the lowly maiden, who was her father's chattel becomes a person of power, able to make a difference in the world. 2) When threatened by the dwarf's

---

[84] For a more detailed discussion of work, see Megill, Thinking for a Living, particularly Chapter 4.
[85] The stages of the Hero's Journey are followed in more detail in earlier sections. This is a brief overview as it is seen in this particular tale.

appearance to claim her firstborn, she calls together the community and gives them a unifying task: to find knowledge, the name of the dwarf. The baby is saved, and a new era begins – the kingdom has a new heir, a new king-to-be, a new ruler, therefore new rules.

If the modern leader is to lead the organization into a transformed work culture this hero will probably not be spared any of the stages of this journey. The hero and organization will undergo a significant emotional event that threatens the life of the organization. The hero and organization will muddle around in a wasteland, a "dense forest" like the brambles that barred the prince from Sleeping Beauty. These same brambles had deterred many a former prince who gave up and turned back home, to the familiar. If the hero accepts the challenge, there will be help from unlikely places – not in the bookstore in a how-to book, not on the web under "road map through the dense forest to Sleeping Beauty." And in the end, the hero and organization will emerge with a boon, a benefit, a blessing, a bounty – a way to transform the work culture into one that fulfills people's highest desire in working: making a difference. One that makes the organization profitable, desirable, and a leader in the community.

For those not satisfied with the bottom-line-only approach, the rest of this chapter goes into more detail on each of the characters and what they might mean both psychologically and in modern life.

A Set of Workplace equivalents – with caveat

Because we are working with symbols and a symbol can never be pinned down to one meaning, giving just one possible equivalent that would make "workplace" sense of the fairy tale is dangerous and misleading. It takes away some of the rich possibility of other meanings. We invite readers to make their own set of workplace characters that could just as legitimately represent the modern equivalent of the fairy tale characters we are about to malign.

That being said, let us plunge ahead into forbidden territory and propose the following equivalents:

The daughter/maiden, a.k.a. queen	=	modern-day worker, whether male or female (with apologies to the male reader)
The miller	=	a sales manager prone to self-promotion
The king	=	a leader prone to greed and self-aggrandizement
The dwarf/ Rumpelstiltskin	=	a consultant prone to hoarding his knowledge
The baby	=	the leader-in-training, the heir-apparent
The community	=	a Community of Practice that works together to produce something of value
Discovering a name	=	appropriating the person's power, depotentiating the person, seeing that person for what he or she is

Now let's see if we can make sense of this tale for modern times.

The Community

In the tale of Rumpelstiltskin, it is the community that accomplishes the task of finding the magic gold-maker's name. The community, by working together on a common mission, pooling their collective resources, and being highly motivated (saving the Queen's baby is, after all, noble work – tantamount to saving the future of the kingdom) finds the answer. One of them stumbles on Rumple high in the mountains, celebrating. Many others bring back interesting names, adding information to the domain of "Names." But one finds the key to the Queen's dilemma.

In reading the literature on communities today, particularly communities of practice, the term is used rather imprecisely. It has come to mean almost any gathering of people. One could even argue, "but look at this rag-tag community the Queen gathered – weren't they just a gathering of lots of different folk?" "Only on the surface," comes the retort. They were unified by their very specific mission: go find the name of the scoundrel who will take the baby. They collected for a time, did their job, shared their findings, then went back to being the butcher, the baker and the candlestick-maker, i.e., no longer a community in the business sense of the word,[86] only an interesting collection of individuals who happen to live in the same village.

One could also argue that the community did not find the name, one person did. What chance did one person, working alone, have of stumbling on Rumpel, the recluse? Or if that person did happen to wander upon a strange little hermit doing a drunken-sort of dance by the fire in a remote mountain spot, what notice would that person have taken? The event had significance only because of the mission of the community: go find every name in the kingdom so the Queen can keep her baby. With that focus, in that context, the event had great significance. No longer was it just an interesting story to tell the grand-kids around the fire, now it was the essential piece of information. It allowed the Kingdom to perpetuate itself. Now, when the old king dies, there is a new king waiting to take over leadership.

Two things, then, distinguish a community: it has a unifying mission and the individual members don't just cooperate, they collaborate – i.e., they work together; they share their findings in order to fulfill their mission.[87] The community of members operates as one organism.

---

[86] See Appendix II for a business definition.
[87] Ken Megill makes a very important distinction between cooperation and collaboration in Chapter 3 of his book, Thinking for a Living. His premise is that collaboration is based on immediate accessibility of information that allows people to work together solving problems. Cooperation is based on each person doing his or her own work but letting others see or have the finished products, when asked, or when scheduled. Assembly lines are based on cooperation. Knowledge Work is based on collaboration.

Community as a symbol for psychological development

The internal "community" can be seen as all the different parts and functions of an individual's psyche.

All of us have a rag-tag army (community) from far-flung parts of the kingdom/psyche, gathered on the hillside awaiting our leadership. Jung gives them quite specific names: anima, animus, shadow, ego, to name a few.[88] We could as easily speak colloquially and name each part of ourselves by something we define in our own peculiar ways: the helper, the martyr, the over-achiever, the bum, the Monday-morning witch, the parent; the list is almost endless.

The goal of real maturity is to get this community functioning in harmony. So that, for example, the bum doesn't take over – except maybe for a while on Saturday mornings as lawn care is ignored in favor of a third cup of coffee and a comic strip – or the overachiever, for that matter, or heaven help us, the martyr. Our real job is to have them collaborate, to work together on a common mission so that one part doesn't thwart the functioning of the whole, doesn't throw a monkey wrench into the works on the very brink of success.

Each part remains very important in its own right. The well-rested bum gives us the energy to return to work, the over-achiever who marches to the top of the hill gets a reward. Our job is to value each member, not to exterminate one, but collect them together, and provide the leadership so that they can function as a community.

The symbol of community today

What happens when the community is involved? They gather information to make knowledge; they fulfill their mission of finding Rumpel's real name. When they name him, he self-destructs – thus ending the threat to the Queen and the loss of the whole community's next leader. Through Rumpel's demise, the Kingdom is safe again.

The community received detailed instruction about its mission. The Queen (boss) had to tell them her dilemma, engage them in her project, and elicit their participation. After all, it meant that the blacksmith couldn't operate the smithy, the baker had to forego his bread making, no candlesticks would be produced for these three days and the washerwoman would leave the village clothes dirty. It was not an easy thing she engaged them in doing. She had to be clear about the challenge and clear about their mission.

---

[88] For a definition of these parts see Appendix II.

Understanding the Tale 89

While they formed this particular community, they were all engaged in the same work. The candlestick maker was no longer forming silver into candleholders. He was now a name-finder. How did the community use his talent? We aren't told, but because time was short, we can assume that the community had to organize itself along lines that made most sense to accomplish the task at hand.

The other crucial part of their functioning is that information couldn't be hoarded, findings had to be shared, even if they seemed "weird." It took courage to report the strange scene in the mountain – surely it wasn't relevant, some little man singing. The mission was too important, though, to leave any name un-nominated. In functioning in a unified manner (collaborating), they created knowledge: an answer to the question, "is this the name of the spinner of gold?"

The creation of this knowledge concluded their task together – and assured the continuation of the kingdom (business).

Moral

- For the leader

If the future is threatened, bring the community together. They have a much higher probability of covering all the ground so that a solution can be found.

Give them a clear mission.

Engage them.

- For the community

Work as one body – collaborate.

Create an environment of trust so that even "weird" hunches can be shared.

Share information – collaborate.

- For the business

If knowledge is the current kingdom in which businesses operate, communities of practice, focused on a common mission are the agents of this kingdom. Their collective effort produces a result that the Maiden, or any single member of the community, working alone, could not.

Before we leave the idea of community, let's take two different looks at it:

The community is the hero

Traditionally the know-how (about what really gets results and which mistakes to avoid) resides mainly in people's minds. In ancient villages, the elders and early professionals like the midwife, healer, and priest passed on this knowledge through palavers under the baobab tree.

Like the elders, the Buddha sat under a tree, the Bodi tree, until he attained enlightenment. We call such an enlightened one a guru, which means one who leads from darkness into light. A guru has a clear vision and serves as a guiding light until the new reality dawns on others, as well. He went from the Bodi tree and shared what he knew to be true.

Later, in Western cultures, people met to debate and exchange the best knowledge under the trees of the village square.

Only recently have we eliminated the trees and moved indoors to town meetings that performed this same knowledge-exchange function.

In the paper-based culture, such exchanges took place at conferences, workshops, conclaves, professional consultations, and meetings – all functions that enabled individuals to share what they knew and all functions that required bringing people together in one location.

The world in which knowledge workers operate continuously changes so rapidly that waiting for the gathering of the best available knowledge at a conference, or meeting the elders under the local baobab tree is hardly practical. We need a new tree, a new way of working together that facilitates the exchange of knowledge that used to happen under the baobab tree, under the Bodi tree, around the village square, or at annual conferences.

In the Age of Knowledge, these "trees" are called communities of practice . . . groups of people brought together through the work they do to capture and spread ideas and know-how in free-flowing, creative ways that foster new approaches to problems.

In the digital world, chat rooms, discussion groups, and collaborative work environments are becoming the new Baobab Tree. Emerging technologies suggest that the exchange route is the World Wide Web, the Internet. The tale of Rumpelstiltskin suggests it is communities. Growing Communities of Practice suggest that both are right.

> **An example of a community that made its own gold**
>
> At the turn of the last century Vienna, like most European societies, was stratified. One of the strata was the cultural elite. In other cultural centers of the period (London, Paris, or Berlin) the leaders of the cultural elite hardly knew each other; they lived in relatively segregated professional, political and artistic communities. In Vienna, by contrast, the cohesiveness of the cultural elite, until the First World War, was quite strong. The salon and the cafe were vital institutions where intellectuals of different kinds shared ideas with each other and mingled with the business and professional elite of the day. At one table you might find seated a journalist, a painter, a politician, a psychologist, a musician and a philosopher – all excitedly exchanging ideas vital to their own art.
>
> The end of the century was a time of almost unprecedented cultural turmoil in a city that was the capital of an almost impossible empire (the Austro-Hungarian), an empire that Morton[89] called "a dynastic fiction, venerable, fragile, superb." And, it was a time in which Vienna's intellectuals produced innovations that quickly became recognized throughout Europe as "Vienna schools," notably in psychology, art history, and music. Similarly, developments of that period in literature, architecture, painting, philosophy, and politics attained international recognition as distinctly Austrian contributions.
>
> from Evie Lotze: Psychodrama Training Manual, Vol.1 p. 62–63. 1990.
>
> This was a loose-knit, non-commercial community of practice of artists, politicians, and intellectuals. They met in mixed professional groups at the cafes and salons to exchange information. Each individual or group took away information from other individuals and groups, reworked it in its own unique ways and created new knowledge. That era saw Picasso's stage designs for Diaghilev ballets; the emerging of new music as Stravinsky's Rite of Spring shook its opening audiences in Paris. In this cultural setting J. L. Moreno took the ideas of the emerging theater of reality and integrated them with psychology – in not at all the way envisioned by Freud or Jung, who attended the same salons. The free exchange of ideas unfettered by the cultural divides extant in the rest of Europe produced an extraordinary new knowledge base for psychology, music, and painting, to name but a few.

---

[89] Morton, F., A Nervous Splendor: Vienna 1888/1889. Boston: Little Brown. 1979, p.6.

The Miller

The miller was historically the first in the community to own and use a machine to do his work. As such he was not quite like the others, who saw themselves as good, honest, hard-working, "hand-working" members of the community. His way of contributing value was suspect because he used a machine, a method the others did not have, to help him – he cheated, in the eyes of the peasants.

In the tale of Rumpelstiltskin, Miller meets the King one day on the road, and wants to make himself look good, so he brags. In fact, he makes an impossible claim – "my daughter weaves so well, she can turn straw into gold." Perhaps he never expected that the King would make him back up this outrageous claim.

It is interesting, too, that he did not put himself on the line. He did not brag that *he* could turn wheat into gold with his machine, the mill. Rather he volunteered his daughter. In this tale he is a bit of a sleaze-bag, befitting a suspect member of society.

The miller as guide to psychological development

The "miller" in us might find little harm in telling a little white lie that will make us just a bit more esteemed to some "king" in our lives. Our own need to look good may get us into a heap of trouble at times – the slightly overstated résumé, the brag about what we can do or have done.

This inner miller part of the psyche might be using some way of producing "flour" that the community doesn't quite trust – might be taking a short-cut path to which others have no access.

The symbol of the Miller today

The miller can be seen as the "hero" of the bureaucrat, the entrepreneur, or the person who owns and runs the business or organization. He finds a way to improve the business process; he shortens the time it takes to do the work; he uses technology to add to profit.

Like the miller, many a salesman or sales manager oversells his staff, creating impossible tasks with impossible deadlines. And occasionally, like the miller, gets caught in his slight exaggeration and puts others in a real bind.

Improvers of business processes likewise promise gold and often, in the process, leave workers distraught, faced by new tasks that they are not properly prepared to do.

Moral

If one function of a tale is to warn of life's dangers or pitfalls, this tale warns, "you are going to cause a heap of trouble from time to time because of your greed, vanity and insecurity; your need to look good, at all costs, in someone else's eyes."

The King

The King is greedy, in spite of the fact that he has everything, including all the power in the kingdom. (Greed is not a rational thing.)

The King is driven by gold. To "go for the gold" is to be driven to achieve the highest possible standard. The king is so obsessed with gold that he keeps the miller's daughter not only the first night, but three nights, escalating each night's task – under the threat of death.

The King can be seen as POWER. Whatever or whoever has the power in a given situation.

In the end, the King has it all – wife, baby, community and the knowledge of the "funny little man."[90]

The king as guide to psychological development

The "king" in us wants more – more money before we can retire, more adventures before we settle down, more time to enjoy life, more toys, more. . . more. . . more.

This inner king also pushes us to achieve our highest potential – our gold.

Psychologically the King can be seen as the ego, the organizing power of conscious life; the one who sees the whole (conscious or known) psychological kingdom. He is the Commander in Chief of the internal ragtag army of characters lolling on the hillside waiting for instruction, waiting for orders that would turn them into a fighting force.

The symbol of the king today

Perhaps most relevant to this book, the King can be seen as the owner, CEO or boss. He knows what he wants, has the power to get it and the power to set consequences for non-performance.

He sets the tone of the culture, in our case of work culture still modeled after the Industrial Age. And this tone is one of greed, use of absolute, dictatorial power. He can be seen as a perfect example of the boss in the Industrial Age.

---

[90] Some readers have objected that the tale does not imply that Rumpel's knowledge of gold-making passes to the King or the Community. In primitive cultures the discovery of a person's real name was similar in meaning to the practice of eating the heart or liver of a respected (slain) opponent: not only was the enemy eliminated, his power now accrued to the victor.

> **Moral**
>
> Greedy bosses can extract the impossible for a time, but in the end theirs is not the glory. They do not usher in the new paradigm; they do not bring about the new culture.
>
> Their power is temporary. Old kings die; new kings can usher in new cultures.

The daughter, or the Maiden

The daughter, innocent victim of her father's braggadocio, victim of the King's greed, despairs.

The daughter begins the story as a pawn of the first industrialist (the Miller). We first meet her after she has been transferred into custody in the King's storeroom.

She pays with the only valuables she has at first – a necklace and a ring, both traditionally symbols of wholeness – (never-endingness, therefore used as treasured gifts or signs and seals of marriage.)

Having given up her treasures, it is perhaps easier for her to make her final deal with the devil, promising her firstborn – the one that carries the hope of the family, the new life, the new possibilities.

In the end, though, it is she who calls together the community and "names" Rumpelstiltskin – i.e., appropriates his power.

The daughter/Maiden/Queen as guide to psychological development

A daughter can be some "young," not yet fully formed, part of ourselves – something to which we've given birth, but will always be younger than we.

In the context of this tale, this might be a part of us born to an "old culture" father, the offspring of an old way of thinking or acting.

The daughter, though, becomes Queen, she grows up, matures – she has used an undervalued part of herself (Rumpelstiltskin) to accomplish an important task and in the process produced something of value (gold). To become Queen is to become the mistress of the realm; all-powerful, master of her own life and that of the community. In other words, the daughter follows the hero's journey, takes the appropriate psychological steps to transform her life and live "happily ever after."

The "miller's daughter" within each of us has been known to give up some treasured value to get some piece of work done. How many Faustian deals each of us has made along the way, giving up a "ring" here, a "necklace" there, but in the end being forced to promise our firstborn, just to get some piece of work done.

As Maidens we all have the luck at times to stumble on the inner resources, often by some brilliant, individually conceived, unconscious "flash of light" (Rumpelstiltskin) that allows us to do the impossible tasks with impossible deadlines. Sometimes simply by burning ourselves out.

Some of we Maidens even become Queen – we get the recognition we deserve as brilliant or simply hard workers and are promoted to posts of high visibility and power.

Some of us also recognize the power and value of community and the help they can render in times of need.

When the miller's daughter in each of us recognizes the situation for what it is (despair at betrayal in this case) and gives up the pretense of being able to get out of this impossible situation by using old, tried, true ways, then help comes to us. This help is not something produced by the ego, not even known or trusted. But, as a result, we are released from prison and become the master of our own realm – for a time.

The second task outlined in the tale is that even as Queen, mistress of the realm, we need community – and must call for and rely on its help. It is the community that accomplishes the last psychological task set forth – the task of rescuing the baby, the potential for something new, a new king, a new culture.

The symbol of the daughter today

The daughter can be seen as an offspring, a product of the first technology-user, a product of the industrial age. She is a worker, one of the properties that the entrepreneur/industrialist/bureaucrat (father) owns.

Like all workers, the Industrial Age entrepreneur sees her merely as a tool to be used, someone who needs to be told what to do, and be told in a way that she will do it. Thinking is not for her, that is reserved for the Miller and the King. They will do the command and control. She will do what she is told to do.

The daughter can also be seen as acting very rationally in a life-threatening situation – a good person to know in a crisis.

One might also see the daughter as the up-and-coming Manager posed with insurmountable difficulties who accepts a guru (Rumpelstiltskin) willing to help.

The daughter is the real hero of this story. It is she who is transformed from lowly Miller's daughter to Queen of the realm, by accepting her situation and the help offered. It is she who is the instrument for saving the kingdom, by calling together the community to save the king-to-be.

> **Moral**
>
> If tales not only warn of life's dangers, but also offer instruction on how to surmount the danger, the instruction in this tale is:
>
> "When you are in trouble, there is help at hand – often you must give up your expectation that the old ways of doing things will work, though, before you can get the help." One life-saving source of help is your community.

The Baby

Throughout world mythology and literature, including the birth of Christ story, babies have represented our new hopes, our future, our possibilities for new life.

This baby, furthermore, is the future King, the heir apparent of the current King and Queen.

When the old King has outworn his usefulness to the kingdom, the kingdom is often portrayed as lying fallow, in dire straits; the crops fail, the people are poor, foreign armies encroach. The renewal of the kingdom comes with the coming of a new, younger, fresher King.

The baby as guide to psychological development

A baby is very newly emerged part of ourselves, one that while not very psychologically developed, nevertheless brings new hope, unknown possibilities.

A baby, particularly one born to the throne, can be seen as not only new hope for psychological development, but a new possibility that, if nurtured – and not lost to the dwarf-thief – will replace the old ruler of the personality.

The symbol of the baby today

What would it mean to save the kingdom of a business world? What is the new hope? The future? The possibility of new life? What is the boon at the end of the tale?

The emerging future new life in the current contemporary business world seems to be one of creating knowledge – if we can transform the culture to support it.

As the new King, the Queen's baby is an excellent symbol of the new culture. With a new ruler often come new rules, new fashions, new ways of acting in a culture. In today's work culture this could mean a new relationship to technology, new relationships in and between communities of practice, new collaborations, new ways of doing work.

Moral

Not all new possibilities, potential growth into a new culture, will come to the throne effortlessly. Some will be lost (stolen or given up.) A watchful, deeply attached "mother" or "ruler" (Queen) is needed to call out all resources of the individual personality or of the business in order to save this creation.

Rumpelstiltskin

Rumpelstiltskin, the little man who solves the problem, as an external figure, can represent a guru, a consultant, or a whiz kid – a miraculous problem solver. He believes that knowledge is power; therefore he hoards it. He hoards both his knowledge of how to make gold and the knowledge of his name. His death is the death of the Industrial Age.

Early in the tale Rumpel is a hero. He is the creative one. He is the one who gets the job done behind the scene; the help from unexpected places. He brings skill and gets things done. He lives by his wits, not by his position or his power in the community. But HE is the one who can actually spin straw into gold.

Later in the tale, though, he is the villain. He demands too much; he demands the firstborn.

He hoards his knowledge. (He does not tell us how to spin the straw into gold, nor does he tell who he is and how he works. He keeps his name a secret.)

Rumpelstiltskin as guide to psychological development

Rumpel enters the scene when the ego (the part of our personality that's supposed to be solving the problems out there in the world) has given up. There is no hope. The task is impossible. Out of nowhere, through a locked door, appears a "little man." All the signs are that this is not a rational, conscious part of ourselves. Like the ants that come to help Psyche when she has to sort the lentils from the pile of millet – or the animal helpers who throughout time have appeared to help the hero solve the impossible, just in the nick of time. Rumpelstiltskin personifies the unconscious help we draw on. The flash of insight that un-knots a nefarious tangle, or the solution to a problem that comes through a dream, or the appearance of a mentor out of nowhere just when most needed.

Obi-Wan or Yoda are wonderful modern-day Star Wars mentors – without the dark side of the Rumpel of the tale. However, it was Rumpel's dark side that evoked the denouement that is critical to this tale fitting the needs of Work Culture Transformation. If Rumpel hadn't threatened to take the new king, the community wouldn't have been called together to create knowledge. If Rumpel's rage hadn't destroyed him, the security of the new heir to the throne would not have been complete.

The symbol of Rumpel today

Help in this tale appears unexpectedly, from a previously unknown source. A dwarf was a character about whom people in early Europe had great prejudice. So the maiden's help comes from a source that was deemed "inferior."

His price is high and continues to escalate. He can demand it because he is the only game in town.

He is an excellent symbol for the old work culture, the information-hoarding culture, but he uses tools in a new way, a way that foreshadows the coming of a new culture. (Computers emerged in the end of the Industrial Age, the spinning wheel emerged at the end of the Agricultural Age. But for a new culture to emerge, they must be used in a new way – as Rumpel used the wheel in a way that made it produce gold.)

Moral

When you need help, it often comes in strange forms.

If you hire someone who will not tell you how he works and share his knowledge with you, you are likely to find yourself over an impossible barrel.

When the price gets too high, find a way out. The way out is through a community – collaborating with a group of people whose mission is your own.

The King's Storeroom

The King's Storeroom is where the king keeps his straw and other commodities he needs to govern and provide for his kingdom. It becomes, in fact, a dungeon when he locks the door and keeps the Maiden prisoner until she performs to his satisfaction.

The symbol of a storeroom in psychological development

The storeroom represents the predicaments into which we find ourselves locked, either through no fault of our own, or because our greedy internal "king" demands the impossible. Our ego says "get off your lazy duff, do more – plant a garden, paint the basement, learn a language, improve your tennis game – more, more, more." Furthermore, the ego symbolically "locks the door" – won't let us escape the impossible demands it makes.

Being locked in the King's storeroom can mean that we find ourselves in a dire situation, particularly in relation to the dominant (King's) culture.

The symbol of a King's Storeroom today

If the King is the one with the dictatorial power and this is his "holding" place, what better metaphor is there for representing the industrial workplace? It is the location where huge tasks await the Maiden/worker. There are deadlines to be met, quotas to be filled.

The storeroom becomes the Maiden's dungeon when she is asked to do what she hasn't got the skills or experience to do. She succeeds, but at enormous personal cost.

Moral

Locked storerooms/dungeons serve the industrial culture's purposes, but only for a time. In the end, the Queen (worker) changes the rules. And remember, the Queen is now co-master of the realm; therefore co-owner of the storeroom.

Straw

Straw is the stuff used for bedding animals and keeping them warm through the winter. It has little intrinsic value and is plentiful, therefore of little worth.

Straw as a symbol of psychological development

Straw can represent that "stuff of life" that has little value – what's left after the wheat is harvested. Wheat nourishes us; straw is only used for lining the stables of animals. It is similar to the lead of the alchemists who tried to make gold. They took relatively worthless material and tried to make it into something of substantial value.

Today it can represent something we hold in low esteem, take for granted and consider worthless.

Our psychological task throughout life is to take the straw and lead that life deals us and create something of value, something worth having, gold.

The symbol of Straw today

Straw in today's business world can be that daunting, despair-inducing mountain of stuff facing each "miller's daughter" on a Monday morning (paperwork, data input, reports that exist in one form, perhaps even on line, but need to be changed to meet another organization's requirements).

It can also be the mountain of data that must be sorted through, evaluated, compared, contrasted and contextualized in order to transform it into knowledge.

Perhaps more importantly though, it is all the rules and regulations, beliefs, assumptions, mores, rituals and expectations (in short, the culture) that prevent us from getting immediate access to the information we need to do our work. The same culture prevents us from openly sharing the work we do with others who need it to do their work.

Moral

Straw, the meaningless, worthless stuff of life can be transformed. The task does not have to be life threatening, despair producing, or overwhelming, but we need help to do it.

Straw is also the parts of the culture that prevent our working effectively on the job at hand: spinning gold, making knowledge.

Get help when you need it – otherwise the King takes your life in the morning.

> **Gold**

The King in the story values this precious metal so much he imprisons the Maiden and threatens her life if her father has led him astray.

Gold was used in ancient times as ornamentation for royalty, later; it came to be used as the medium of exchange.

Gold as a symbol of psychological development

Gold symbolizes finding what is the best – in ourselves, in our work, in our culture; our highest value, the most precious part of our world and ourselves.

Our gold comes from very unexpected places (a dungeon, a locked storeroom of straw) – often only after the ego gives up – after the tears.

Gold is the first boon in the story (the baby is the second). A very suspect character helps the hero produce this boon.

The symbol of Gold today

Today's gold is no different from the gold of the medieval world in which the tale was written, or the earlier time in which myths were created. When Jason was sent to retrieve the Golden Fleece, he was sent to find the best.

The highest honor in the Olympics is the Gold Medal.

In today's business world Knowledge is our Gold – the thing we value, the stuff we work to earn, the highest achievement. It is what we train and pay our people to produce. It is the "coin of the realm."

> **Moral**
>
> You can get the gold from the room of straw (from the old culture) but the price is very high and comes through a very unusual source of aid.

The Spinning Wheel

The spinning wheel was the tool the Maiden used in her work, an ordinary, household object used on a daily basis.

The Spinning Wheel as a symbol of psychological development

Our normal way of working, a tool we recognize for getting work done. If a spinning wheel were to appear in a modern-day dreamer's imagery it would possibly represent an old way of seeing our work, using an old tool, one now out-of-date.

The symbol of a spinning wheel today

The spinning wheel was a familiar tool, the mode of production of thread; a way to transform wool into thread. But in the hands of Rumpelstiltskin it was used in a different way and transformed straw into gold.

Today, we can use computers, a familiar tool to do work in the Industrial Age manner – with a boss breaking down the work into smaller and smaller pieces and parceling those pieces to workers who then return finished products to be assembled by the boss. Workers in this system hoard their knowledge of how to produce their piece of the work, thereby protecting the future of their jobs.

Or, we can begin to use this tool in a new way. This tool has the capacity to allow us to collaborate in a community of practice and get a new product, knowledge, which we have described as today's gold.

Moral

If we are using tools in an old way, and expect to spin straw into gold, it won't work. We must find Rumpel's power (his name) in order to use this tool differently, as he did to spin gold.

For those who are willing to read a myth or fairy tale with the "third eye" and see it as symbolic and not just an interesting story to entertain children, each character can bring to mind someone we have known. For those who are prone to think psychologically, the characters and other symbols can be recognized as parts of the psyche of ourselves and those we know. Their actions become recognizable and spark revelations about our own process of transformation: "Oh, yes, when I lost my company I spent a long time in despair, feeling like a failure. Then I met that guy on the bus, the one who wrote children's books. Three hours, a missed bus stop and a cup of coffee later, I had an idea for my first book. Now that's what I do, I write children's books. Go figure!"

For workers and leaders who are caught up in or thinking about a transformation of the work culture, reading Rumpelstiltskin with the "third eye" can produce similar insight into the process of transforming an organization.

SECTION V

Getting on with the Transformation

In which we describe symbolic equipment for the journey, play with the idea of an organization's transformation process by using a psychodrama setting – and then summarize in a more straight line fashion.

Seeing with the "third eye"

This section makes demands on the reader to use not just the thinking part of the brain, but to use the symbol-making, story-weaving, imaginative part as well. We call this seeing not just with the two eyes adorning the face that take in information from the "real" world, but seeing, as well, with a "third eye" – one that can see things the other two don't.

The section describes symbolic equipment that will help the hero make the journey successfully. It also takes a look at the process of transformation in a hypothetical organization. To telescope a long and complex journey that in reality might take a large organization a year or more of concentrated work, we'll use an imaginary psychodrama stage to represent the process – besides; it's more fun than pages and pages of linear description. But to witness this imaginary psychodrama vividly will demand of the reader the use of the "third eye" – that whole-picture, intuiting, imagination-seeing "eye."

We all have the ability to see the big picture and to see the details. Some of us are better at one than at the other. Likewise every organization has what it characterizes as big picture people and detail-oriented people, each serving a valuable function. For the moment, I ask the reader to become the big picture person. Suspend disbelief until all the pieces are in place and the big picture emerges.

> Twelve men were blindfolded, led to an elephant and asked to describe the animal. One's hands found the tusk and described the animal as having a smooth long, hard, sharp body. Another, having been placed at the elephant's side, declared that this was a large, fat animal with rough skin. Still another, from the ear perspective, said, no, this is a thin animal, very pliable. The blindfolded "observer" at the trunk insisted that this was a snake-like animal.
>
> Blindfolds removed, they realized that the details taken together, while right, still did not give an adequate description of the animal they now saw before them.

The process of seeing with the whole brain also involves thinking symbolically rather than literally. See the possibilities, not just the facts as the story unfolds – see it with the "third eye," for it is the images that speak here, not the individual words, or even the individual "problems" to be solved.

CHAPTER 10

Equipping for the Journey

In which we hope to make time-tested tools and methodology available to the modern hero.

Even Hercules had to equip for his labors of transformation. His journey was launched when he accidentally killed the King of Ithaca's wife and children. The Delphic Oracle assigned him 12 years' service to the King of Ithaca as penance; at the end of which his reward (boon) would be immortality.

To help him in his labors, the gods gave him a sword, a bow and eagle-feathered arrows, a breastplate, a robe, a team of horses and an unbreakable shield. These gifts of the gods, the active, (sword, bow and arrows, and a team of horses) and the protective or passive (breastplate, robe, and shield) helped him make his journey triumphant.

Have no doubt about it; transforming to the work culture of the Knowledge Age is a Herculean task. An ordinary mortal will need to equip for the task in no less thorough a manner than Hercules himself did – except that in Hercules' case the gods did his equipping; probably we will not be quite so blessed.

This is a risky trip. It will not be as magical as kissing a frog. The frog-kisser is just one side of the equation. Think about it from the frog's point of view: incredible demands are made on his body and mental processes as he is transformed into a Prince. Although the frog has already gone through one transformation, from being a tadpole, to reach the elevated state of froghood, we can assume that he is ill-prepared for this frog-to-prince venture. In other words, he's had practice and experience transforming, but that doesn't make the process easy.

A well-equipped hero is one more likely to make a successful journey and return triumphant – even though he is spared none of the stages and their attendant difficulties and confusion – just like the frog. The modern hero who would take on work culture transformation knows (and fears) that the journey is arduous and messy, that it is not something that can be rationally planned and neatly project-managed. The modern business hero is an adventurer, not unlike Columbus, embarking on a journey for which there is no map. But the gods have given the hero gifts of active and passive natures that will make the Herculean task survivable. From the heroes of old the modern hero can intuit what equipment to take on the journey.

Protective armor – the breastplates, robes, and shields for the journey:

Knowledge as armor

It helps to know where you are going on the journey. The modern business embarking on a journey of transformation needs to be clear about its vision, its mission and its goals. It helps to know what information the workers need in order to do their work and what information they will be producing in doing their work, for the Knowledge Age requires that both be immediately accessible (to those who need it to do their work). A business that has done this part of preparation for the journey is better equipped to take the journey. Workers who have been included in the preparatory process weather the storms of the journey better than those who are not so armored.

It helps to know what to expect of the road, as well – forewarned is forearmed goes the adage. Imagine a passenger with a bad back riding in an automobile. When the passenger knows a bump is coming, the back can be braced appropriately to lessen the impact. The rider knows just how to brace, knowledge gained from years of jostling along rough roads.

We need to go into the journey forewarned of what lies ahead; in place of a road map, we have powerful stories of those who have taken similar journeys. These stories serve to inspire, to instruct by example, to help us warm up to the task ahead. They show us the dangers; they promise success if our attitudes and actions are right. If we are to meet the cyclops, pass through the gates of hell, do battle with demons, or be hung on a meat hook, how shall we survive?

Myths and tales of old let us know that we are not alone and that many others have jostled their way down the bumpy road we are on. They tell us how those heroes acted, what they did and did not do (how they braced themselves) in order to survive their bumpy road.

The story of Rumpelstiltskin had a heroine with no armor; she was taken completely off-guard. Her father's braggadocio resulted in her life-threatening incarceration. She had no knowledge of the journey – that it would bring trials beyond her capacity, that help would come at the darkest hour, and no knowledge that in the end she would receive a boon. The comfort that that knowledge could bring was missing to her – she was on her own – and wept in despair.

What we know about the journey (from Section II)

1 We will be "jerked" out of familiar ways of doing things by some cataclysmic event. Our response is highly charged. In other words, the journey will not be the result of a calm, rational, intellectual decision to "change." Change may happen that way; transformation does not. Transformation is fundamental, qualitative, wrenching – and surprising.
2 We will encounter monsters, swamps and pitfalls that cannot be foreseen and for which there are no known road maps or cures.
3 We will get help along the way, but that help will not come from places we know, expect, or even respect. The help we get will enable us to successfully battle the monsters.
4 If we persevere: (i.e. accept the challenge, slay the monsters, escape the swamps and pits, and accept the unlikely help that is offered) we will return home with a boon – but home will now be a different place. For our modern hero this will be a transformed work culture – a new way to do work.

Attitudes as armor

Not only knowledge of what to expect on the journey but the attitudes we bring to it will help us complete the trip successfully. From myth and tale we can gather some of the attitudes that helped other heroes:

Devotion (Loyalty)

When Beauty learned that the cure for her father depended on one of his daughter's going into the forest to live with Beast, she went. Her motivation? Devotion to her father. When Psyche, struck yet again by her curiosity, opened the box she was to have delivered unopened, Eros, overcome by his love for her and his compassion for all she had been through, rescued her. His devotion overcame her foolishness. The modern hero, as well, will fare far better on this journey equipped with an overarching loyalty to those involved in the journey ahead. Why else

112 *Getting On With the Transformation*

take on this impossible task? No abstract, intellectual concept will sustain a journey into territory marked only with the warning "here lie monsters."

Trust

Whether one reads earlier versions of Cinderella or the Fairy Godmother version, Cinderella needs an inordinate amount of trust. Picture an untrusting Cinderella, disappointed at not going to the ball, confronted by a spirit who promises her the world – easy enough to dismiss without a second thought, except maybe one of seeking out medical help. Or, consider Jack who meets the magical-bean peddler. How much safer to proceed on to the market and sell the cow at the going rate. He'd have returned home with enough money to buy the next month's groceries, maybe. His trust resulted in the never-ending supply of golden eggs. Consider Noah and God's ridiculous request, one sunny day, that he build an Ark. An untrusting Noah is portrayed by comedian Bill Cosby[91] as saying something to the effect of "Yeah, right, God. A big boat, right? In the middle of this desert? And what's a cubit?" To such a dumb request, the only self-respecting response is to question and reject as untenable. An untrusting Noah would have resulted in no rescue of all the animals two by two and a world overcome by flood.

The modern hero who accepts the call to adventure is called upon to trust. Trust that she/he will get the help, trust the unlikely helpers, and the monster-slaying tools in his equipment. When the boon is presented, the hero must trust that, too. It may appear to be "just a box" – one that needs to be investigated, at that. Or a bunch of beans.

Trust becomes invaluable in the Knowledge Age, as workers must depend on accessing information rather than relying on reports generated at predetermined intervals. They must trust (and be able to trust) that the information they get is the latest and most reliable on which to base their work.[92] Without this trust they will revert to the old way of doing work. Rather than "look over the shoulder" of the co-worker, they will interrupt the work to ask for proof or verification.

A Zen approach to doing the work: Chop Wood, Carry Water

When Snow White, lost in the woods, came upon the diminutive house, curiosity led her in and her sense of doing what had to be done led her

---
[91] a popular U.S. comedian
[92] See the Work Culture Assessment in Appendix III for a fuller discussion of Trust in the Knowledge Age

to begin to establish order in the dwarves' house. Zen masters through the ages when asked what one does after enlightenment have responded, in effect, do the work at hand: chop wood, carry water.

This is good advice for the journey, as well as for actions "after enlightenment" in the world to which one returns having retrieved the treasure. We return, transformed, re-energized, revitalized – and must still walk upon the ground, one foot in front of the other, doing the next thing to be done. For example, when knowledge workers begin to replace reporting with access, what does this mean? How do you do it? Chopping Wood, Carrying Water seems to suggest that you just do it – begin to give access to web tools and work done on the web rather than send reports – hopefully with the full support and pre-planning of the organization and its leadership.

Awe

When the fisherman caught a fish that spoke to him, he was awe-struck. Even before the fish promised to grant his wishes (and not limited to a restrictive three, either), the fisherman knew he had caught something numinous (awe-inspiring, shining with an inner light). He was so smitten that the experience was its own reward. He asked for nothing more. (Not so, his wife of course, and therein lies the tension in the story of the fairy tale. The moral of the story is that greed leads to self-destruction, but that's a different point.)

A sense of awe about the business of transformation, helping midwife the frog to a prince, is an appropriate stance for the modern hero. The journey itself is awesome (sometimes awful – full of awe) and the help that emerges "out of the blue" can leave one feeling amazed and reverent – awe-struck. And sometimes, you are left with the feeling, "'awe-shucks' – is that all it is? I knew that all along."

A trusted ally

The earliest myth known to modern folks is that of Inanna. When she made a dangerous journey into the underworld, she left word with her trusted colleague that if she did not return in three days, the colleague should go to the gods on her behalf. Inanna had incomplete knowledge. She knew that the journey would be dangerous, but she could not plan for the particular dangers, so she made provisions for her return. In fact, when the colleague arrived, she found Inanna hanging (but alive) on a meat hook, a rather graphic image for the sorts of dangers that can lie in wait for us on our journey. An ally can "find us when we're lost." We can trust an ally to bring us back to the known world, to the light of day, to ground us when needed.

In an organization undergoing transformation, allies within the community and outside help us "keep our heads screwed on straight," think through things, create solutions to impossible situations, and rescue us from the alligator-infested swamps.

A community of co-adventurers

Sometimes we take more than one ally on the journey. When Jason set out on his adventure seeking the Golden Fleece, he was accompanied by many fellow travelers, the Argonauts, each skilled in his own right, knowledgeable about the sea, tested warriors, trusted companions. They helped meet the trials, slay the monsters, win the battles *and* collectively, they knew the way home. What one forgot, the others could supply. Likewise in the Odessey, it wasn't up to Ulysses' aging brain alone to remember, create, or manage every turn and twist of the route. Neither will modern heroes have to do all of the work of transformation of a work culture – if they are in a community, or in several of them. Make of them co-adventurers. Co-adventurers cover your bases when you can't; they cover your back when there's a showdown at the OK Corral at High Noon. They function for the CEO, the president, the manager, the worker in the same way they functioned for Jason – together they found their way through the threshold, through the wilderness, to the goal and back again.

Markers: stones over breadcrumbs

Hansel, meaning to mark his way home, dropped breadcrumbs along the way – only to discover that hungry birds unwittingly obliterated his trail. The white stones that would reflect moonlight were a much more reliable trail marker. If the modern hero has no trusted ally or community who can help with the return home, then our hero should take a pocket full of stones to mark the return trip. Stones are permanent, immune to the pecking of hungry birds; they endure and reflect the light. In modern parlance our "stones" might be things of permanence like books, articles, training, communities of practice, or web-based knowledge about this journey of transformation, about culture transformation, or about the possibilities for the modern workplace. They provide ideas, guidance, lessons learned, and hope.

Action on the journey: the swords, bows, arrows, and teams of horses

A sword

Our hero needs some tools for action. A sword is a fine symbol of a hero's ability to act in his own behalf and on the behalf of others in the community. If we turn to mythology's most famous sword, Excalibur, we learn from Arthur's tale that all the strongest and wisest in the kingdom, all those with aspirations to be King, had tried to extract the sword from the stone. Arthur was a young man/boy with a simple, unassuming background. He did not set out to become King; he saw a sword, needed a sword, so picked up this one that was handy – only later did he learn that he was a King. May we all be so fortunate to find a handy sword for the taking and one whose rock releases it when we need it. Surely this is an example of help from an unexpected place.[93]

A modern organization's sword might be a leader with the power to cut the red tape; someone brought aboard the transformation journey by the enthusiasm of the vision. It might be someone from the mailroom with the ability to see the bigger picture of where the company is going and willing to take the risk to break with tradition. It might be a charismatic change agent from some unlikely corner of the organization who finds solutions to problems that others haven't thought of, tried or had the technological wizardry to accomplish. Swords are found in unlikely-looking stones.

Creativity, more unexpected help

In myth and fairy tale, the help that comes from unexpected places often arrives in the form of an animal, the wind, a talking river, insects, a bird, a fish that talks.[94] Heroes are those among us who have developed access

---

[93] An interesting side line of the Arthur story is that only those not so deeply imbedded in the existing culture (the wisest and strongest in the land) will be able to extract the sword that will propel the culture into new directions – the next generation of leaders. The young Arthur, after all, united the kingdom, brought about peace and introduced the culture of chivalry – a culture transformation that lives in legend today. Not bad for a boy brought up far from the world of royalty and power.

It was a young Luke Skywalker who saved the day with his light saber, a sword only wielded by the Jedi Knights. Every Jedi Knight had to create his own sword – as will each modern hero. It is up to us to make our sword, for we are not normally as fortunate as boy Arthur, who came from the right stock, without even knowing it.

[94] Remembering that all characters in the tales are externalized parts of the hero (ourselves), these helpers can be seen as symbols of unconscious aspects of ourselves.

to the unconscious. Which is another way of saying that they have access to the creative function.[95] Jung, who thought and observed a lot about the process of creativity, says that it often appears when we are at our lowest mental level. Traditional heroes often become heroic when the functions they usually rely on are not working well – often in times of great stress.

For modern heroes one source of creativity is the by-product of calling together a community of the best minds, spirits, skills and experiences from their field and others tangentially related. The power of web tools enables us to call upon members of communities who were not accessible before – or were only accessible through luck. It is often still luck, but a much bigger pool of it – the luck of community members. Often the most creative communities are made up of people from disparate fields, like the butcher, the baker, the candlestick maker and all the other searchers the Miller's Daughter/Queen called together. Communities may systematically make or serendipitously find the creative solution to the problems we face.

Focus:

In the myth of Eros and Psyche, Psyche is sent into the underworld (Hades) to retrieve a treasure box. She is given barley cakes, two coins, and instructions not to stop for any reason. Even though she meets a starving man, a beggar who needs coins and a dying man who needs help, her critical instructions were all designed to keep her focused on her task. If she were to be distracted, lose her focus:

- she would not have the barley cakes to feed Cerberus, the three-headed dog who guards the entrance to Hades,
- she would not have the coins to pay Charon, the Styx ferry man to carry her back from Hades, and
- she would have missed her boat had she stopped to help the dying man.[96]

---

[95] Creativity can be accessed, discovered, or developed – or it may simply appear.
[96] The cost of her own survival in the underworld was that she did not share a barley cake with a starving man, perhaps hastening his death. She did not give a coin to a beggar, perhaps increasing his misery; and she did not help the dying man, perhaps hastening his death, as well. There is always a cost for our individuation, a price too high for many to pay. Many are the would-be heroes who get distracted providing temporary relief to a starving man, beggar, or the dying.

For the modern hero, as well, focus is critical. Keep your eye on the goal: find a way to create the culture that will get the work done. There are many ways to keep one's eye on the goal – write it down, stick it on a wall, paint it, envision it, picture it, put numbers to it, make it as real as possible. Bill Clinton is said to have put a sign on his campaign office wall: It's the economy, Stupid – to remind him of the focus of his presidential campaign. Not to keep one's focus, warns the tale of Psyche, means to get trapped in Hades.

Curiosity, the hero's team of horses

All the heroes of myth and tale have a sense of curiosity. Sometimes it led them, sometimes it drove them, but each had it. Psyche's curiosity launched her adventure. Jack's curiosity about the magic beans led him into the Giant's realm, in which realm lay his boon. Bluebeard's wife was curious about the key and the forbidden room. Sleeping Beauty was driven to her wilderness by her curiosity about the forbidden activity of sewing. Each hero, driven by curiosity, was called into adventure from which each emerged richer than before.

Curiosity about the unknown is an attribute of mind that propels the modern hero, as well. "Why is it we have always done things this way?" "What would motivate people to collaborate?" "How will I engage the whole staff in this transformation?" "Look at this roadblock. How fascinating. I wonder how we'll get around this one?" The curious mind wonders about the unknown and looks for surprising things. If you are curious, finding what you expect would be a disappointment.[97]

Each of the heroes explored in this book, mythic and real, accepted a call to adventure; wandered, lost, in a wild place; found unlikely help; and returned triumphant. How did they do it? They put on the armor of community, trusted allies and their knowledge. They marked their way home and they did what had to be done. They picked up the sword of creativity and focus. They took with them the attitudes of an open mind: devotion, awe and curiosity.

---

[97] For example, psychotherapists who work with dreams know to probe past the known to find the surprising. Dreams, being part of the journey to transformation, never come to tell the dreamer what the dreamer already knows – they reveal something of which the dreamer is not yet conscious.

CHAPTER 11

What Do We Do on Monday Morning?

In which we get somewhat practical on the topic of how to begin the task.

Go to work and be a Hero – do the real work of moving the wall[98] – the wall that confines the present work culture. Recognize that you are an ordinary person who has received the Call to Adventure – however inelegantly it was delivered. Accept the call; take the next step, realizing that you are embarking on unknown territory, but with a goal.

The call was delivered to Cinderella through the death of her mother; Hansel and Gretel through abandonment in a deep and dangerous forest; Ulysses through the Trojan War; and Psyche by being thrown out of her marriage condemned to wander from one impossible task to another.

Modern heroes may launch their journeys in response to the death of someone close, a life-threatening illness, political oppression, revolution, or the loss of home or business.

If you are the recognized leader, prepare colleagues, workers, fellow leaders and the business community in which you operate for the journey, as well as yourself. Frame the journey for those who would join you: workers, co-leaders, colleagues, the business community. Write, speak, lead, set the example; this helps others equip themselves for the journey. Those affected by your leadership, in your company or in your world will

---

[98] Herb Schantz, a brilliant engineer who pioneered OCR technology, defines Work (he always says it with a capital W) as moving the wall. One can push it all day, he says, do it elegantly, with good will and creativity – but unless the wall moves no work is done. He reminds us that in physics, Work equals force applied over distance (W = F X D).

undertake a similar journey of transformation, but be affected by it in their own unique ways. Let them know about the lack of signposts along the way in this strange land that they are about to enter. Alert them to the existence of trials on the way. Tell them to expect monsters and roadblocks in this wilderness. Make them ready to accept aid from unusual sources – sources they never credited in the past. Hold out the hope of the boon for those who will undertake the journey and stay in the process to its end. In other words, give them a larger perspective than that of chaos from which to view the process on which they are about to embark. In short, engage the community – remembering it was the community that saved the kingdom for the Queen in Rumpelstiltskin and rescued from obscurity and entrapment its new leadership.

For both individuals and organizations, accepting the call begins the journey to transformation and the boon it brings. It is dangerous, but if we have the right armor and swords and leave markers along the way, we might survive – and even return triumphant.

Projecting Ahead

Put yourself forward in time – far enough for the new work culture to be firmly established, for philosophers to be announcing that the Knowledge Age is about to give way to the next revolution.

At the end of the Knowledge Age, as yet another emerging age throws its shadow on the horizon, sages of the transformation process may look back and say, "Here is the road map followed by those heroes who led the last transformation." Just as today, in retrospect, we can look back at the Industrial Age and point to critical bends in the road and shifts in the culture that we now call the Industrial Revolution. Those caught up in the chaos of that transformation often went reluctantly into it, not knowing they were in any particular part of a larger picture that was slowly resolving itself into clarity.

Future philosophers and map makers may be able to say in their perfect wisdom: They took path 1, which led to road 2, they avoided the detour through the swamp en route to interstate 3 and so on to successful termination.

At this beginning point of the journey, though, we are still thinking a little, planning a little, deploying a little, learning a lot. However, even with our limited vision of the future, we can find ways to start our journey because we have a destination in mind. We know the potential that technology holds, we know the roadblocks industrial culture throws up, and we know that the culture needs to be transformed. Furthermore,

What Do We Do on Monday Morning? 121

we know the stages of that transformation. The way might not be straight; we might have to go places for which we do not have a guidebook or a map.

Besides, it is more fun to wander than follow a straight and narrow path – or at least it is a better adventure, or so Little Red Riding Hood assures us.

The uncharted territories can be the most rewarding ones of all for we will not only be heroes but discoverers, explorers and adventurers. Few are lucky enough to spend their lifetime as professional explorers, so bringing about a transformation in work culture can be fun, as well as satisfying (and a bit scary at times). We set off into uncharted territory with a rough-drawn map marked like those of old "hic sunt animales" – here be monsters. The well-armed heroes of vision, like Christopher Columbus or the Vikings, will land on the shores of a New World.

The leader who would like to, or is compelled to, transform a work culture to one in which people achieve their highest potential and the company reaches its peak of productivity and profits has a daunting task. Other leaders may be tweaking the process, providing leadership training to promising new workers, assuring that change management techniques are widely known, and making sure his or her workers have all the latest bells and whistles. They may well be shaking their heads at our poor hero, thrown into the journey toward transformation; it is so "impossible to achieve." But in the end, it is the hero who returns with the boon, the benefit, the blessing. It is the hero who has a culture that supports collaboration in communities of practice; it is the triumphant returnee who has cut the Gordian Knot[99] of compensation for knowledge workers who do not occupy an office or work regular 9–5 daily hours. It is the wanderer of wildernesses who has tapped the creativity of colleagues and workers to design a system of work that works for all – from the shareholders to society at large, for the company's profit and the workers' benefit. It will be the modern hero who has tapped the wellspring of development – and shifted the experience of the basis for reality in the work culture. Workers will bring to work a new set of expectations, a new "common sense" about how things get done; they will see reality differently.

A Left-brained summary

We have asked left-brain-dominant people to take on the whole brain function, think symbolically and metaphorically, and see the big picture.

---

[99] King Gordius of Phrygia tied a knot that could only be untied by the next ruler of Asia. Alexander the Great cut through it, solving the problem quickly and boldly (and in violation of all the rules).

122 Getting On With the Transformation

It is only fair to ask right-brained people to take on the same whole-brain function and to focus now on the details, the facts, the specifics of the process of transforming the work culture.

The process of work culture transformation involves four stages:

1 An external event that throws the organization into the realization that it can no longer do business in the old way.
2 The organization has an inevitable period of chaos adjusting to the external emotionally laden event.
3 When help comes, it comes from unexpected, unlikely and un-respected places.
4 The end of the process is a transformation that brings new energy into the organization.

Communities, some would call them Communities of Practice, are the agents of work culture transformation. Forming/identifying communities requires three steps:

1 The organization must identify its mission and the work required in order to reach that mission.
2 The community that does each piece of the work in the organization must define the information it needs in order to do its work successfully and define where that information can be found.
3 The communities and organization must make information (both the information they produce and the information they need) immediately accessible to those who need it to do their work.[100]

Communities have three characteristics. They work collaboratively, which means that

1 to co-labor the community **shares** information,
2 they **trust** that the information of their collaborators is the best and most current, and
3 they **preserve** the knowledge it creates for re-use.

---

[100] For an excellent discussion of Communities and the Methodology of Transformation see Megill *Thinking for a Living*, chapter 6.

What Do We Do on Monday Morning? 123

Implied in these three elements is a great deal of community "care and feeding."

> *"Knowledge creation and knowledge transfer" (are) "delicate processes, necessitating particular forms of support and 'care' from management . . . . Knowledge must be 'nurtured' rather than managed."*[101]

Sharing, trust and preservation of knowledge for re-use are not magical fall-outs of having "formed a community." They are hard-won and continually re-created.[102]

Work Culture Transformation means fundamentally changing the way we do work. It will be more productive, more profitable, even more satisfying and fun – but the process is not easy, not short, and not manageable in the ways we now recognize.

---

[101] Knowledge Emergence. Social, Technical and Evolutionary Dimensions of Knowledge Creation. Edited by Ikujiro Nonaka and Toshiro Nishiguchi, Oxford 2001, p. 4.
[102] See the Work Culture Assessment in Appendix III for more detail on these three aspects of the culture change.

CHAPTER 12

Transforming a Business Psychodramatically

In which we telescope a long, messy process into a theatre production.

In this chapter we will use an imaginary psychodrama to summarize or telescope the long and arduous process of transforming a business. By using an imaginary psychodramatic session to condense the process, let me assure readers who are also decision-makers in an organization that by using this method of summarizing we are not suggesting that the best way to transform an organization is necessarily to hire a psychodramatist. Psychodrama might well be "help from unexpected places." But the main thrust of this book suggests that heroes, whether they are individuals or communities, are thrust by extraordinary events into the journey of transformation. They may take allies and co-adventurers with them, they may go armed with shields and swords, but they must take the journey for themselves.

A hero's psychodrama

Let's imagine for a moment a very successful organization[103] that:

- Has a clear and exciting vision of its mission and purpose;
- Has a very strong team of very smart people. They all like their work, share the vision of the organization and know where they and their work fit in;

---

[103] There is a particular successful organization that was very much in my mind when I created this psychodrama. It is the same organization that is the subject of the survey in the appendix. I owe a great deal to the people who work at that wonderful organization.

- Has all the bells and whistles: systems in the organization function reliably, work smoothly and talk to each other;
- Has streamlined all its business practices.

But something's still not right. They can't seem to take advantage of the 21st Century. The technology is there, but the work is still being done in the old way because the world hasn't changed around them.

The troubled organization could as well be a company that comes seeking advice for other reasons:

- the loss of a big customer,
- a powerful executive steals from the company,
- new technology rendered the business obsolete,
- or any other modern scenario that leaves the organization saying, "this is a mess, we can't go on this way."

These scenarios may be easier to dismiss as, "well, that certainly doesn't apply to me." Therefore, I've chosen a successful organization to illustrate how transformation occurs.

In effect, it is usually the experience of the Call to Adventure, the disorientation produced by some catastrophic event, that brings people and organizations alike to the consulting room.

The Call to Adventure, as we saw above, can take many forms. What makes it a Call is that it comes from beyond our control – whether from an outside event, or one internal to the company such as embezzlement or poor management. The important point here is not the particular facts of the case, but the process that occurs when transformation takes place.

The impetus for transformation comes from forces beyond us – from the father offering up the daughter to a greedy king. That offering can take many forms, but from the viewpoint of the daughter, it makes little difference.

The offering may also have little or nothing to do with the individuals in a situation, but be aimed directly at the institution, the business or the organization in which work is done.

Organizational transformation, like individual transformation, follows the same pattern and the same ebb and flow.

For that reason, one way we can understand and experience transformation and what it means is psychodramatically. The organization takes the problem – the situation – to the psychodrama stage. Once the organization comes to the stage, our drama might proceed something like the following (although how it proceeds in any given drama is not so important as the understanding of transformation that emerges).

A drama has a director. In the case of psychodrama the director is not someone to tell others what to do – or even to direct. The director is a guide, a coach, someone who provides structure when needed, clarification, and helps bring about satisfying closure. This person may be trained in transformation and may assist others in the process, but transforming a work culture is not a drama, it is real life and does not require a director or coach. It does require people taking hold of their situation, confronting it, accepting where they are, and being creative.

The organization is the protagonist. An organization, however, has no voice, but speaks through people who may lead the organization or may play any number of roles. What is important for the process to work is that those involved take in the "big picture" – assume the role and place of the organization. In order to do so, they need to believe that when they do that it will make a difference, which is why transformation requires leadership from those who manage and direct the organization. The transformation process requires that not only leaders be involved, but that the community be involved. The community will include many natural leaders or leaders who emerge because of their expertise and experience in different areas.

Once the organization begins to speak, perhaps those involved might choose to select one or more people to articulate the situation and represent all those involved. Those playing the role of the protagonist consult with all those involved to list the frustrations that brought the group/organization to the psychodrama. Each frustration is only one strand of spaghetti. Not until there is a whole plateful will there be a satisfying meal.

Scene I: Accepting the Call

In all the following scenes, unless otherwise indicated, the organization is the protagonist, the person who has stepped into the role of the organization and speaks in the first person.

Like readers of this book, this protagonist is familiar with the process and stories of transformation.

We start with where we are. We accept the Call. We welcome the challenge. We may be afraid, but we step out, not knowing where we are going. We can't go on like this. We can't do business this way. We are maidens thrown into the storeroom, life threatened unless we can do the impossible.

128 *Getting On With the Transformation*

Director[104]: Let's see the scene. As if this were a theatre stage, show us how it is. As each member of the organization thinks of one of the frustrations facing you, step forward and assume the role of that problem and give it a voice.

Members step forward, one at a time, and speak:

- "Another organization wants a report, but the boss won't go to the URL and download it for himself, wants someone to send it to him in a very agency-specific format."
- "I need information from a vendor in order to submit a bid. But I don't have the right user identification and password. The procedure for getting one is so complicated it will take me a week to get it and they need the bid this week. I shouldn't have to put up with this – just let me write my proposal."
- "I got a R.F.P. (request for a proposal) but it came in as gobbledy-gook. I don't know what stone-age program they were using. Four telephone calls later and they finally faxed me the thing and I had to scan it into our program."
- "They've given me a sexy new program, they say, but I'm on my own to learn it. It is not intuitively obvious and we're out of training budget. Even if we had budget, I have no time to go across town to training, with a huge group, march lock-step through it, only to forget most of it by the time I need it."
- "Half the time I come to work, my technology doesn't work, it is still Neanderthal, I can't get my work done. I spend my time duplicating information, spinning my wheels and I'm still getting straw."
- "The information I need to do my work is not available because of "rules" that govern my relationships. I can't go into my client's data base and work with him to get this job done."
- "Joe down three cubicles just did the same sort of project. You know when I found out? At the Christmas party after a 70-hour week of reinventing the wheel he'd just patented."
- "We can make significant changes within the company. We're pretty savvy folks. But the rest of the world is just not cooperating. I feel like

---

[104] This is one of the places the director steps in to get the ball rolling, to help the group start a process that is not natural to them – enacting situations to find different solutions than those that present themselves in meetings. The director will have helped structure the talk about why the organization is here and provide methods for choosing of different roles and voices in the drama. The director will also ensure that a variety of voices are heard and that many group members experience many of the different perspectives to maximize creativity.

Don Quixote, tilting at windmills all whirring furiously in the wind of "the way things are."
- "Everyone thinks the project of changing the world is just pie-in-the-sky. Or, worse yet, people think changing the world is great as long as it is other people's world that changes and not their own.[105] How do we change what we do not control?"
- "Yeah, but, you know we could tackle each one of these problems by themselves. But even then we wouldn't be working differently. Not the way we see it can be done! We can practically taste a new way, almost touch it. But we can't get there."

Director: You seem to be struggling against a whole culture. Like the popular version of Columbus' voyage (that tells us his men rebelled against travelling further, least they fall off the edge of the flat world), you *know* that the world is flat. You want to believe this vision of Christopher's, but you've had no experience that would justify that belief. You haven't sailed forth yet on the Nina, the Pinta, or the Santa Maria.[106] Your beliefs remain in the realm of intellectual ideals, hopeful dreams, and philosophical rummaging.

A change of this magnitude amounts to a transformation. You'd barely be able to recognize the world that would solve all the situations you've just articulated.

The curtain closes on Scene I with the acceptance of the Call. With that acceptance is a recognition that there are no solutions in sight – at least no easy solutions. There is little we can do but wander about lost in a wilderness of details that "just aren't working." (This is the point of the journey at which the Israelites, wandering in the wilderness, begin to grumble to Moses and make themselves a golden idol.) In other words, they recognize that they may lose many of their fellow travelers in this wilderness, particularly if it goes on for the proverbial 40 years – so they try to recreate what they have known before – the golden calf.

Scene II: Wandering in the Wilderness

The scene opens with the players on stage beginning to talk together, identify solutions, contract for change:

---

[105] A few examples: A commanding officer of a large unit orders those under him to replace reporting with access, but still wants to be briefed himself. A large consulting company is hired to transform the units of a large government office, but the central office is to be left alone. A parent brings the family into therapy with a long list of changes – that others must make.
[106] Christopher Columbus' three ships on his first voyage to the New World.

130 Getting On With the Transformation

- "We know how to solve each one of these problems"
- "This process looks like the Quality Improvement Circles that the organization used 10 years ago. We identified problems, rooted out causes, and put improvements into place. The organization knows that this is a good thing to do – maybe even a necessary activity – but in the end, lots and lots of time was spent on quality improvements that were, in the end, pretty obvious."
- "But we know in our hearts that we will not change the real situation. New frustrations with technology, training, rules, old ways of thinking will just pop back up and eat up all the productive time."

After some time spent wandering about (sometimes called brainstorming), the group is encouraged to begin to think metaphorically. They go back to the tale of Rumpelstiltskin to see if it will help. In that tale, the community found the solution to the maiden's problem and rescued her by discovering the name of the consultant who had helped her out of her dilemma. They begin to look at the characters in the myth and take on various roles . . . one becomes the Maiden, another Rumpel, another the King, and another the Miller.

The King riding in his coach in the forest, meets the Miller. After some chit-chat, he says: "I've got the ultimate power over your world. I am the owner, the Joint Chiefs of Staff, the CEO, the Executive Director, the Big Cheese. I set the wheels in motion."

Father: "I can enrich your kingdom. I have a special daughter. She is beautiful, good and very talented. Why, she can even spin straw into gold. There is little she can't do for you."

King (eyes light up): "I'd like to meet this wonderful young lady. If she is as good as you say, we will both benefit."

Father (to daughter): "Have I got a deal for you – make you rich and famous."

Maiden: "That's your trip, not mine,"

Father: "I've got power over your life. I've got the cosmic two-by-four. I can make your life miserable. All I have to do is promise that you can get that airplane off the line and in the air in record time and under budget. You spin the gold"

Maiden: "You treat me like chattel. I'm your "resource" to assign. You promise the moon and give me a tricycle to get there. You lock me in and throw away the key."

Father: "Yeah, but you'll become the wife of the King. You'll have glory and power."

Maiden: "You've done it again. Your big mouth has made trouble for me. Why does this feel so familiar? How did I wind up victim again?

I know my job as spinner! But this wheel can't do what you're asking. How do I get out of this one, and why is it me losing my life because of your braggadocio?"

Father and King exit, new best friends. Maiden is locked in her room of straw with a spinning wheel.

Rumpelstiltskin enters: "Why, sweet maiden, whatever is the matter?"

Maiden, weeping: "I can't do it. He wants gold by the morning and what he's given me is straw and an old spinning wheel for making thread."

Rumpel: "I can help you – but it will cost."

Maiden: "Anything. Ring? Take it. Necklace? What good is it to me now? Baby? What's that but a dream? Real is – I am going to lose my life."

As the story unfolds, many different group members have stepped for a time into many different roles. One person playing the role of Father realizes that a simple statement meant to ingratiate himself with the powers that be has imperiled the life of his daughter, an unintended consequence. Another in this role has a sudden insight that as supervisor; he has assigned impossible tasks because he did not consult the workers. Which insight comes is not the point. What is important is that seeing the whole picture from different angles produces different perspectives about problems and solutions. (The role of the director is to help the story unfold and to encourage the actors to make asides, as in theatre, that reveal what they are thinking and feeling but not necessarily saying as part of the action. This allows for modern parallels to be told that are not strictly part of the fairy tale.)

The scene now fast-forwards to post wedding of King and Maiden, enters the baby, the community, and our old friend, Rumpel.

The group has described the Rumpel character as short, ugly, warts on his face, talking funny, demanding the impossible, and doing things mysteriously – and not showing them how to do them. It seems he practices black magic. They are afraid of him and don't like him much.

The group agrees that they neither like nor trust Rumpel. They also agree they are over a barrel. For this scene they have chosen the organization's consummate bureaucrat, a boss whose only job seems to be to make their lives miserable, but he's in a position to do something and is under pressure "from above" to turn the situation around.

Rumpel (in his mountain hermitage has heard of the birth of the baby) soliloquizes:

"I've got what they want. They are just too stupid, lazy, and inept to go out and get it. I've got POWER and it's mine, all mine. Carefully locked in my cave, it is, high up on this mountain. Now, all I need is my baby, a little human company, one I can mold in my image."

His rage at being discovered and having the secret name, where his power lies, revealed brings the realization that he – and therefore, each of us – is vulnerable to having our life changed irrevocably by a change in technology, a shift in the market, or a change in circumstances.

The community is perhaps the most interesting part of the drama. First the hero (the organization) must define what work it does to meet its mission in order to define who is in the community. (Keeping in mind there may be many many communities. For the sake of telescoping the transformation process into the confines of one drama, we will use only one community; one chosen by the assembled group.) Defining what work is done means defining what information the workers need to do that work. Those who have the information needed to do the work are members of the community. As the organization struggles to put a community on the stage, they know that defining the work and the information needed to do the work will take a lot of hard work, but for the psychodrama they begin symbolically to represent the people from different worlds who are part of the problems facing them:

- Organizational heads with whom the staff interfaces, from whom the staff needs information and who need information from the company in order to do their work.
- Customers
- Vendors/suppliers
- Stockholders
- Problem-solvers, change-agents, and dreamers within the company
- In short, all those who rely on the company and on whom the company relies.

As they play out roles all members of the organization throw in ideas, and try some out – audience and players exchange places and roles throughout to get different perspectives. A scene of creative chaos ensues as people try new ways, new "rules." We begin to see that the solution for our problems, like the problem faced by the hapless maiden, must come from somewhere quite unexpected.

Scene II closes with the band of travelers – now a community – still in the wilderness, but they are creating new signposts, slaying dragons, finding armor and swords. They are ready for help from unexpected places.

Scene III: Help from Unexpected Places

Director: Where can we, the organization, find unexpected help? Just as we identified problems in scene I, we need to keep our eyes open for really unexpected help – help from unorthodox places, from unusual people.
Many participants offer ideas:

- "Well, for example, there is a "gatekeeper" in our organization who makes sure that we never quite know what is going on. What if that person became a hero?"
- (General groans all around . . . "But he's such a jerk," calls someone.)
- "What would it take to empower that person to become an information sharer instead of an information hoarder?"
- "What if we did away with training and instead had performance centered learning?"
- "We can set up a number of communities of practice and begin to identify what we know and find our strength in each other."
- "What if we gave up trying to "master" technology and instead shared what we know about what we have?"
- "None of us really know how to use our tools . . . and we don't have the time or patience to learn. What if we set up systems and procedures where we praise and reward one another for teaching and sharing our mastery with others?"
- "What if we each showed someone something new every day . . . .and learned from someone else?"
- "What if we identified members of our community outside our organization and reach out to them and bring them into our world? This means leaving the office, both figuratively and literally – going out into the digital world and making contacts, nurturing them and using them to instill fun and excitement into our work."
- "What if each of us made a point of NOT working in the office for extended periods of time and each of us tried out new ways and places to work. This means that everyone will have to get really new ways to get information if we can't walk down to the cubicle and expect to find someone there. We will have to begin to work on the web and enable our colleagues to look over our shoulder as we work."
- "What if people were paid for what they produce and not how much time they put in?"
- "These are all preposterous ideas and not at all realizable unless we change the way we work, the ways we think about work, the prejudices we bring to work – really change them and develop a new work culture based on information sharing rather than information hoarding."

Help can come in many forms: from their own staff, their own tools, or their own ideas. It need not come from an outside consultant, a guru or an author. But it could.

Scene IV: Equipping for the journey

Hero: What if I equip this team for the journey?" Turns to the group, asks them to choose the armor and weapons (for a reminder of what they are, see Chapter 10) they need for the journey.

Each member chooses what he/she most needs to set out on a long wandering in the wilderness, meeting the unexpected.

They remember the Call to Adventure; the cosmic two-by-four, the possible loss of the organization, and they re-enter the wilderness. This time they are equipped. They know what lies ahead: swamps, no guide posts, monsters and help they will not want to trust.

General hilarity as they encounter the monsters, armed now with the gifts of the gods to Hercules. When they emerge, each describes the end of the journey, the boon they find.

Scene V – The boon

A return to Scene I, but with things working. Organization members who can see this newly emerging way of working with their third eye, step forward and speak:

- "We've invented a new way of working. Everyone works on the web."
- "I've developed relationships with the people who create the information I need and trust them enough to be able to look over their shoulder and get the information I need without asking for a report."
- "When I can see the latest work in progress, I know it is the most current possible information to use in the work I'm doing."
- "I've got a relationship with that jerk who always wanted special reports. Now I don't even need to give him a URL. The information he needs is immediately accessible to him on my network."
- "I'm working with vendors. We don't just cooperate, but we work together. He's no longer a salesperson or a supplier. He's a part of the community. He plays an important role."
- "Customers are part of the workplace."
- "Everyone understands how their work relates to the health of the entire organization. All work is done with an eye on the customer. And

every staff member, regardless of role and function, develops relationships with customers so that their needs are met."
- "We've got a transparent organization. Middle management is no longer needed. It simply melted away. All those folks are now doing more interesting things."
- "We no longer have a training program. It is gone. We have a learning organization.[107] We learn as we work and we learn not only what we need to know to do our job today, but also what might help us in tomorrow's jobs. Learning and knowing and discovering is a part of our everyday life. We share what we know with each other. We have performance-centered learning modules available so when we need to learn a particular set of skills we can do so – on line and when needed, with access to a knowledge person who can help us out ... a short instant message away."
- "We created a *real* integrated digital environment. Contractors and the organization share information that they need to do their work. We don't need to go through a bureaucracy to share. We just share among those who do the work, both for the organization and for contractors."
- "We have a corporate memory system where we can find what we need to know. We are rewarded for using the knowledge of those who have gone before us and work with us. Instead of constantly reinventing the wheel, we welcome our past and our environment."
- "The owner/keeper of information is identified and held responsible for its timeliness and accuracy."

For in the end we go back to the beginning, but with a difference. We now know ourselves, the process, and how to make a difference.

And we know that once the destination is reached, another call to another adventure will be issued, inelegantly, again. We will spiral through another wilderness, meeting other dragons, finding help in distasteful places and in the end, those who answer the call will emerge with a boon – a gift that makes the world a better place.

---

[107] See Appendix II for definition.

Epilogue

In which we tell why and how myths and fairy tales always have happy endings.

Happily Ever After – give me a break

Myths and fairy tales are stories cultures told around the campfire to address particular challenges that each member could expect to meet in life. They were stories that instructed members of the tribe on how to successfully meet the challenges and transcend the various psychological stages each meets on the road to maturity.

Each tale usually addresses one major issue. When that issue is met in a particular way, the end of the tale is a happy one, expressed in "and they lived happily ever after." So, for example, if a young man is in his developmental "frog" stage – being a particular toad in the eyes of the society – he is instructed on how to "grow up," how to become a prince. After he has successfully become a prince, the happy ending to that phase is that he marries the princess – and lives happily ever after.

What that particular tale does not do is to address the next major issue the prince and princess will face. It does not tell the reader what happens when, after the wedding, the princess discovers he won't pick up his socks; the prince discovers that she burns the toast and doesn't scrape it the way mom did. That's another tale entirely. That tale will begin again with "once upon a time . . ." There will be another mountain to be climbed, another dragon to slay, another witch to bake . . . and if each of these challenges is met in a mature way, there will be another happy ending.

But alas, life continues to offer up challenges. The hero doesn't get to rest long, or sometimes at all – remember poor Ulysses' 10 years of war and 10 wandering, encountering one-eyed cyclopses, singing sirens, and lotus-eaters – and all this after a long war.

And so it is with work culture transformation. An organization might be faced with a change in technology so drastic that its former mission is rendered obsolete. The successful organization will launch into the hero's journey, well equipped with knowledge of the process. It will traverse the wilds of unknown territory, encounter strange beings, some of whom will help them on the journey. They will use Hercules' gifts of the gods to slay monsters and protect themselves from danger. They will emerge at the end with communities that function to take on the next mission. If they are lucky they will live happily ever after – for awhile. Until the next challenge life throws up to serve as yet another call to yet another adventure.

The destination is never reached – or reached only temporarily. Might as well enjoy the journey.

APPENDICES

APPENDIX I

In-a-nutshell Cheat Sheet on Myths and Fairy Tales[108]

In which we give a thumbnail sketch of the plot of the tales and myths in the book.

ALL THOSE TALES IN THE BOOK THAT YOU THINK YOU SHOULD KNOW AND DON'T[109]

Arthur and Excalibur

Arthur was the illegitimate son of the King, Uther Pendragon, who, on the night Arthur was born, sent him to safety with Merlin the Wizard. From the beginning Arthur's life was in danger because he had been conceived in trickery and treachery. One of Uther's loyal knights raised Arthur unaware of his heritage. When the old king died and the land was in search of its new king, legend had it that only the person who could pull the sword from the stone would be king – and that king would unite the kingdom. Arthur had no reason to believe that he would be that king. Imagine his surprise when the sword slipped easily from the stone in which it remained solidly entrenched as all the best and brightest, as well as the kingdom's scoundrels, tried to free it.

---

[108] These are not the Walt Disney versions of tales where all the difficulties and unpleasantness is removed. The difficulties are the very heart of what calls us out of our complacent lives – they are the whole point and essence of the tale.

[109] Readers may notice the ethno-centricity of my allusions to myths and fairy tales. While Joseph Campbell and Dr. Jung studied the tales and myths of all cultures, often reading them in the language in which they originated, I have focused on those of my own culture – and often despair that I have mastered even those.

Beauty and the Beast

A rich widowed merchant had three daughters. One day his ships were lost in a storm and the family was forced to move out of its fine home to a country cottage. After some time there was news that some of his ships had washed ashore in a neighboring town. The merchant asked each daughter what she wanted him to bring when he returned. Two wanted the finery of their other life, but Beauty asked him to bring her a rose, for that was what she missed most. Alas, the cargo was sodden and worthless; the ship was a wreck.

Returning, the dispirited merchant, not able to afford a place to sleep, was lost at night in the deep woods. When all hope was gone, he spied an alley of trees untouched by the snow that fell in the woods. As he approached, the gates opened to him; inside he found warmth, a sumptuous meal spread for him and a warm bed. In the morning he found a suit of dry clothes and a magnificent steed prepared for his journey home. Before leaving the palace, he picked a rose for Beauty, whereupon a magnificent roar erupted from the palace and a terrible Beast appeared, demanding his life for disturbing his garden. The merchant pleaded that he be excused for having picked a flower for one of his daughters. The Beast bargained with him that he could take the flower and send him a daughter to live in the palace. The merchant promised to return, himself, after delivering the flower.

Beauty, however, would not allow her father to die because of a flower he had picked for her and insisted on going to the palace. Life at the palace evolved pleasantly for Beauty and she grew to enjoy her dinners and conversations with Beast, except that each night he asked her to marry him. She replied that alas, she could not.

One day, Beauty saw in a tower mirror that her father lay ill; she asked to be allowed to go to him. Beast permitted it, but made her promise to return before the crescent moon had turned full. Beauty's father recovered under her care and her jealous sisters pleaded with her to stay with them, knowing the Beast would be furious if she did so and punish her.

One night Beauty dreamt that the palace was dark and cold and that Beast lay dying. She immediately returned and indeed found it so. Her tears and sorrow revived the Beast when, of her own accord, she promised to marry him and live forever in the palace with him. For now she knew she loved him, he was immediately transformed into a handsome prince.

In a pique, a fairy had cursed him and the entire palace for having placed too much value in appearances. She changed them all into animals until someone would love them for their other attributes.

Bluebeard

There was once a very rich man with the misfortune to have a blue beard that made him so ugly that women ran from him. He wooed the youngest daughter of a neighbor with such lavish parties that she began to think that his beard was not so blue, after all. She consented to become his wife and mistress of his fortune. Shortly after the marriage, he had to take a trip, but wanting his wife to be happy in his absence, gave her the keys to his treasure rooms, banquet rooms, and apartments, imploring her to invite her friends and party in his absence. By the way, he added parenthetically, this smallest gold key, the one to the little closet on the ground floor, must never be used.

Guests came, admired the lavish furniture, feasted on the sumptuous food. But the new wife left them and went to satisfy her curiosity about the forbidden closet.

When her eyes adjusted to the dark room, she saw that she was standing on a floor covered by pools of blood and surrounded by walls covered with the headless bodies of former wives. So great was her fear that she dropped the key. She hastily recovered it and dashed from the room to recover from her fright. She tried to clean the blood from the key, but it would not oblige.

Bluebeard returned unexpectedly and asked for the keys. Discovering her infidelity, he ordered that, since she was so anxious to go into the closet, she would join the other wives.

She was unable to melt his hard heart with her pleading, so begged for time to say her prayers. She made her loud prayers from her tower hoping her sister next door would hear and send her brothers to her aid.

When her time was up and the sword at her throat, her brothers entered and ran their swords through the would-be assassin, leaving the new widow to inherit the vast estates of Bluebeard.

Cinderella

Cinderella's tale of woe begins when her mother dies and her father remarries a woman with three daughters. The father is gone frequently and the stepmother wickedly relegates Cinderella to tending the kitchen, where she is always covered with the soot and cinders of the fire. One day the King announces a ball to which all the eligible young women in the land are invited, so the Prince can choose a bride. Cinderella must sew the dresses for her stepsisters', but she is allowed to attend only if she can sort the bowl of lentils her stepmother threw into the fire and the ashes. Distressed, she goes to the Hazel tree she had watered with her tears at her mother's grave and wept bitterly. There, the little bird that nested in the tree (some versions say it was the Fairy Godmother who answered her distress, but the Grimm brothers tell it otherwise) calls on all the birds of Heaven to help her sort lentils from ashes. She then calls on them to provide her a golden dress, silk slippers – and she goes to the ball. The Prince falls madly in love with her, but when he wants to escort her home, she runs away and escapes into her father's dovecote. The second night of the ball, the same scene repeats itself, this time she escapes to a pear tree. By the third night, the Prince is wise to her and has the stairs coated with pitch. While she manages to escape, she loses one of her shoes in the pitch. When the Prince scours the countryside for the Maiden whose foot fits the shoe, try as the sisters might, including cutting off some toes, none of them can don the shoe. The Prince insists that even the cinder maid try the shoe, so Cinderella washes her face and hands and comes out to put on the shoe and become the bride of the Prince. On the wedding day the birds that had helped Cinderella pecked out the eyes of the stepsisters. Such are the wages of wickedness.

The Fisherman and his Wife

A fisherman caught a flounder that spoke to him. The flounder was an enchanted prince and asked that the fisherman spare his life. The fisherman, delighted to have met a talking fish, threw it back into the lake. When the fisherman returned to his hovel, his wife asked him if he'd caught any supper. When he told her about the enchanted prince, she demanded that he return and ask the prince to grant them a nice little cottage to live in. The prince did so and it was not long before the wife escalated her demands, first to a mansion, then to a palace. Then she wanted to be King, then Emperor, finally Pope. Each time the wearying prince obliged. When she demanded to be like God, the prince balked and told the fisherman to return to his home, where he would find his wife sitting in their original hovel – where they sit to this day.

The Frog King

One day the princess was playing with her golden ball, her favorite plaything, and it slipped from her hand into the pool "so deep that its bottom could not be seen." She cried so hard that a frog popped his head up out of the water and asked why she was crying. When she told him, he offered to fetch the ball for her. She offered him her jewels, her clothes, even her golden crown – all of which he refused. He asked only to be her playmate, her friend, to accompany her at the dinner table, sleep in her bed. Not believing for a minute that he could do these things, she agreed to "anything, anything at all." When she tried to renege on her promise, her father admonished her that she must always keep her word. That's how the frog became her companion, her dinner date and her bedmate. When he demanded – and received – his goodnight kiss, he transformed from the bewitched frog into a handsome prince.

Hansel and Gretel

A poor woodcutter and his wife lived in a land devastated by famine and did not have enough food to feed the family. The wife suggested that they take the children to the woods and leave them there to fend for themselves. Hansel overheard his parents arguing about this "solution" to their problem and crept downstairs to find stones to put in his pockets to mark the way home. The second time the children were taken into the forest to be abandoned, Hansel marked the way with breadcrumbs – which the birds promptly ate. This time they were truly lost in the deep woods. As they wandered around, they found a house made of gingerbread, which they began to eat. The seemingly harmless witch invited them in, then evilly captured them into cages where she began to fatten them up to eat. But again, clever Hansel tricked her by poking out a chicken bone when the near-sighted witch wanted to check his fattening-up progress. Finally, the witch, impatient for the tasty meal of roast child decided the time had come. She made Gretel get out to build the fire on which to roast Hansel. Gretel pushed the witch into the roaring fire and let her brother out. They searched the witch's house, found her chests full of pearls and jewels and hitched a ride home across the lake on a duck – where they were joyfully received by their newly widowed father.

Inanna

The Sumerian goddess Inanna left the "great above" where she ruled as Queen to go to the "great below," to the netherworld, the land of no return which was ruled by her sister Ereshkigal, whom she feared would put her to death. She left instructions with her trusted messanger to go plead her case in the hall of the gods if she had not returned in three days. At each of the seven gates to the underworld, Inanna, as custom demanded, removed a piece of her clothing and left it there, so that at the last gate she entered the underworld naked. The judges of the netherworld fastened their eyes of death upon her and she hung from a meat hook for three days. The trusted messenger arrived, as promised, with dirt from under the fingernail of a god that became the help Inanna needed. Help from a very unlikely source, indeed.

Jack and the Beanstalk

Jack was the only son of a poor widow. When they were down to their last piece of bread to eat, his Mom sent Jack to market with their last remaining resource, a cow. On the way to market, Jack met a man who offered him a handful of magic beans in exchange for his cow. Jack made the trade and returned home to show his prize to Mom. In fury and desperation, Mom threw the beans out the window and sent Jack to bed without any supper. When Jack arose the next morning, his room was in the shade of a giant beanstalk. Jack climbed to the top and found the castle of a Giant whose wife befriended him and helped him hide from the boy-eating Giant. As he narrowly escaped from each climbing of the beanstalk, he took with him a treasure, for which the Giant chased him to the edge of his kingdom. On his last visit he stole the Giant's hen that lay a golden egg each day. This time the Giant continued chasing Jack down the beanstalk. Jack, being more nimble, reached bottom first, found his ax and chopped down the beanstalk, causing the Giant such a fall that he created a huge crater. Jack and his mother, however, lived well on the hen's golden eggs ever after.

Jason and the Golden Fleece

Jason, when he reached his majority, went to request the crown of Thessaly, rightfully his, from his Uncle Pelias. Obliging, Uncle Pelias suggested that before Jason assume the throne, he embark on a journey to regain the Golden Fleece which rightfully belonged to his family. To undertake this journey Jason asked Argus, the greatest shipbuilder of the time, to construct for him a mighty ship (the Argo) to carry 50 such luminaries as Hercules, Theseus, Orpheus, and Nestor bent on the adventure for the Fleece. These heroes became the Argonauts who consulted the sage Phineus on how to navigate the impossible passage between the Clashing Islands, yoked fire-breathing bulls to a plough, and sowed the teeth of the dragon that Cadmus had slain. From these teeth sprang a crop of armed men programmed to turn on their creator. These the Argonauts slew with the help of a charm from Medea, the daughter of the king. Jason charmed the ever-alert dragon that guarded the fleece, escaped with the fleece and returned with Medea and the Argonauts to Thessaly, where Jason took his rightful throne.

Little Red Riding Hood

Once a little girl's mother dressed her in her daring-beyond-her-years red cape with hood and sent her out into the wolf-infested woods to deliver a basket of goodies to her ailing grandmother, with the instructions that she was to stick strictly to the path. She was further instructed not to speak to the wolf. Little Red set off on her journey and soon was tempted by all the wonderful spring flowers. She wandered just ever so slightly off the path to pick a bouquet to add to the basket of goodies for her granny. Well, one flower led to another and soon she was well off the straight and narrow and into the woods.

She was startled to hear a voice address her, "Top o' the mornin' to you, m'dear. And where might you be headed this fine day?" He was so polite and so civil that she was surprised to see that this was none other than the wolf himself; Mom must be mistaken about him.

She replied that she was off to see her grandmother, who lived in the wee cottage at the edge of this very woods. The wolf commented on how thoughtful she was and asked if she knew the other path that would take her there – the one with all the wonderful flowers that would add such a nice touch to the bouquet she was making. Whereupon the wolf proceeded by the shortcut and Little Red took the nice-touch-flowers path.

When she got to granny's house; the wolf had eaten the tough old girl and hopped into her bed to deceive Little Red. When she had asked her many questions about her "granny's" appearance and had just finished commenting, "Granny, what big teeth you have," the wolf sprang out of bed to make dessert of Little Red.

Luckily, Little Red's father, the woodcutter, was nearby, heard her screams and dashed to her rescue, slaying the wolf and releasing Granny from his tummy.

Psyche

The story of Cupid (Eros) and Psyche (Love and Soul) is one of a lifetime's struggle to unite the two. Psyche was given in marriage to Cupid, in disobedience of the wishes of his mother, Venus. The one condition Cupid imposed was that she not gaze on his face, or even ask to see it – she must love him as he was, neither adoring him as a god, nor fearing him as a demon. Provoked by her jealous sisters' taunting that she must be married to a monster, she broke her promise. A candle she lit to see his face dripped wax and awakened Cupid, who fled. Psyche, in trying to follow him, fell from a window of the castle into the dust below. After years of grieving and wandering, Psyche went in great fear directly to Venus, who told her she was so ill-favored that she would make a trial of her housewifery. Whereupon she was taken to a storehouse of Venus' temple and told she must sort a mountain of wheat, barley, millet, vetches, beans, and lentils into separate stacks. Psyche, in her despair, sat defeated. An ant appeared, sent by Cupid to take compassion on her. The ant directed his army of six-legged subjects who made short work of sorting the grains into separate stacks. The river gods who instructed her though the whispering reeds aided her on her next impossible task, gathering the Golden Fleece from rams bent on destroying mortals. Her third trial was to go into the underworld to ask Prosperine for a box of her beauty for Venus, who had depleted her own supply in tending to her ill son (still ill from the candle-wax burn).

On her trip to the underworld she was to take two pieces of barley cake, two halfpenny coins in her teeth, and sufficient strength and dedication to her task to pass up a lame man and a drowning man – both in need of her help. One of the barley cakes she threw to Cerburus, the three-headed dog who guarded the underworld. While the three heads fought over the one cake, Psyche passed safely in. She paid one of her coins to the ferryman, Charon, to cross the river Styx. She ignored both the lame and drowning men and avoided even the temptation to help the Fates with their weaving of human destiny. She obtained the box of beauty and retreated by the same pathway. By disobeying yet another crucial prohibition: that of leaving the box closed, she was overcome by sleep – which, in the underworld is deadly. Eros came to her rescue, admonishing her once again for her curiosity, and pleading her case to Zeus who made her immortal.

Sleeping Beauty

Once a King and Queen so rejoiced at having a child that they invited all the fairies of the realm to the christening – well, almost all. One, whom had not been seen for 50 years, they believed dead, so did not invite. When christening day arrived all the fairies appeared, including the Ancient One, the uninvited. In her pique, the Ancient put the curse of death by spindle-prick on the baby Princess. One of the good fairies had the last wish and unable to cancel the Ancient's wish, modified the death part of it to a sleep of 100 years. The King, thinking to outwit the cruel fairy, had all spindles removed from the castle. But alas, with the curiosity of a 15-year-old, the Princess found one day a spinner using a spindle, which she demanded to try. She immediately pricked her finger and fell into a sleep of 100 years – she and every member of the castle, except the King and Queen, who, after all, had a kingdom to rule. Immediately a great forest, penetration of which was blocked by briars and brambles, grew up around the castle. But, as fate would have it, 100 years later a dashing young prince came upon the castle. Having heard the tales of its history. He hacked through the briars with great perseverance. Great was his reward when he found the beautiful princess "sleeping" on her couch and kissed life back into her body. (The original Perrault version of this tale adds a second chapter of an ogress Queen mother who had her son's new wife and children killed and ate them, only to learn later that a soft-hearted cook spared their lives, substituting wild animals and tricking the Queen. When the son, now King, returned, the Queen mother threw herself into the caldron of vipers she had prepared for the duplicitous cook, Sleeping Beauty and her two children. – A must-read horror tale.)[110]

Snow White and the Seven Dwarves

Snow White's mother died shortly after she was born and her stepmother would not tolerate anyone more beautiful than herself. As Snow White matured into a beautiful young woman; her stepmother plotted to be rid of her. She instructed her huntsman to take Snow White to the forest and kill her. The huntsman took pity on the young woman, killed a boar and returned to the Queen with the boar heart and liver as proof of Snow White's death. Snow White wandered deep into the forest and found the cottage of the seven dwarves who adopted her as their own. But, mean-

---

[110] Opie, Iona & Peter. The Classic Fairy Tales. London: Oxford University. 1974.

while, back at the palace, all was not well. The wicked stepmother asked the mirror who was fairest of them all, and the mirror replied that Snow White was fairest. Enraged, the Queen, knowing she had been duped, donned the dress of an old peddler. She went peddling pretty laces in the forest. When Snow White bought one, the "peddler" tied it around her neck so tight that she fell down seemingly dead. The dwarves, however, found her in the nick of time and warned her to be more careful next time. The mirror reported faithfully to the Queen's next inquiry that Snow White was still fairer than she was. Her second plot for Snow White's demise involved a poisoned comb, from which the dwarves also rescued Snow White just in time. Her third plot, after the mirror's continuing insistence that Snow White was the fairest in the land, involved a poisoned apple. This time the dwarves could not revive her, neither could they bear to put her in the ground; so they fashioned her a glass coffin. There she lay until a prince happened upon the coffin and begged the dwarves to carry it to his castle. They tripped in the process, dislodging the poison apple bit from Snow White's throat, returning her to life. And the Prince and Snow White lived happily ever after – particularly after the evil Queen was brought red-hot iron slippers at the wedding feast and forced to dance in them until she fell down dead.

Ulysses

Having fathered the idea of the Trojan Horse by which the Greeks gained entry into Troy, Ulysses (Odysseus, in the Roman version) began his odyssey home. His interminable trip home took him through one uncharted territory after another: through battles and storms, to the land of the Lotus-eaters and the island ruled by one-eyed giants, Cyclopes. When Ulysses and his men sought to re-provision themselves from a Cyclopes' cave it cost him four men, eaten by the keeper of the cave. In revenge, Ulysses and his men got the giant (Polyphemus) drunk, put out his eye, tied themselves to the bellies of rams and escaped the now blind, but enraged Polyphemus' detection. He later came into possession of a leather bag of harmful winds, which his curious colleagues opened, loosing the winds against themselves and dooming them to further labors and wanderings. After many adventures, Ulysses reached home, where his wife Penelope had been fending off suitors for 20 years. Aided by his son Telemacus, Ulysses killed the suitors and resumed the throne.

The reader is referred to these sources for the full richness of these tales:
Bulfinch's Mythology: The Age of Fable, The Age of Chivalry, Legends

of Charlemagne. New York: Harper & Row, 1970. (For a more detailed synopses of myths).

The Complete Fairy Tales of the Brothers Grimm. New York: Bantam, 1987.

Opie, Iona and Peter. The Classic Fairy Tales. London: Oxford University. 1974.

Kramer, S. N. Sumerian Mythology. American Philosophical Society Memoirs, Vol. XXI; Philadelphia, 1944, p. 86–93.

APPENDIX II

A Platform for Leaping into the New Language

In which we provide some help with words that are used in specific ways in this book.

Ken Megill has provided most of the definitions in this section. The exceptions are the psychological terms; those are a creation of the author.

Anima

The feminine aspects of a male psyche; often used as synonymous with soul. A man's artistic or intuitive gifts may be part of his anima.

Animus

The male aspects of a woman's psyche, the part of a woman that helps her enter the world of work, the traditionally male part of the culture.

Ba

A Japanese term used by Ikujiro Nonaka to describe the environment and culture in which work takes place. Ba is the context that makes a safe haven for the creation of knowledge.

Community

Communities are groups of people who work for a common purpose within an organization or across organizational boundaries. A community, traditionally understood, has a shared place or geography, a characteristic which is not necessary for digital communities.

Community of Practice

One of the new terms that help us understand and conceptualize knowledge work. A community of practice is a group of people bound together by a common class of problems, common pursuit of solutions, and a store of common knowledge and understanding.

Culture

A culture embraces the common understandings, language and ways of acting and other assumptions shared by a community. A work culture is the "common sense" that pervades the workplace.

Data

Data are the facts or raw material that make up information.

Ego

The ego is that part of the personality with which we identify ourselves. The ego in Jungian psychology is the center of the conscious personality, before the process of individuation has integrated more parts of the unconscious into the whole. The Self then becomes the center of the whole. Ego is the Latin word for "I."

Heroes

A hero is a person who is thrust into an extraordinary situation and does not duck the task. A hero rises to the occasion. A hero puts one foot in front of the other and does the best next thing that has to be done.

Individuation

The process of moving from an immature psychology into a mature one that unites all parts of the personality into a whole. There are usually many iterations of the hero's journey involved before the process can be said to be complete – if ever it can be said to be truly completed.

Industrial Age

The industrial revolution came when machines began to drive the productive process. Manufacturing brought workers together in large factories. With the steam engine and other machines (including computers), production began to be driven by the machines and the needs of the machines. A new kind of work took place based on cooperation.

Information

Information is processed data – it is the building blocks used by people when they create knowledge. Information generally requires data to be managed and processed – just as knowledge requires information to be managed and processed.

Information management

Information management is concerned with the acquisition, documentation, arrangement, storage, retrieval and use of information.

Integrated digital environment

An integrated digital environment is a work environment in which there is immediate access to the information needed to conduct business (to do work). Such an environment requires an information-sharing work culture, digital tools, connectivity, and corporate memory.

Knowledge

The traditional philosophical definition of knowledge is that it is justified true belief. Davenport and the Prusaks, the developers of knowledge management define it as "A fluid mix of framed experience, values, contextual information, and expert insight that provides a framework for evaluating and incorporating new experiences and inform-ation."[111]

Knowledge Age

The "fourth wave" – The age of work in which the production of knowledge is the chief productive activity. The Age of Knowledge follows the Information Age, which is the final stage of the Industrial Age, the Manufacturing Age, and the Agricultural Age. How we name the ages is not as important as recognizing that a fundamentally different way of doing work is becoming a reality.

Knowledge management

A methodology for making comprehensive, relevant information (current or historical) available in a timely manner for users (knowledge workers) to make timely valid decisions that increase the productivity of a business application (where a business application is a set of work processes).

Knowledge Manager

A knowledge manager is someone who knows who the experts (knowledgeable people) are, and how to access their knowledge. A knowledge manager is not the same as an expert. An expert functions within a community. An expert is recognized as the one who "knows" more than other people do about a particular topic. An expert is the creator and developer of knowledge. A knowledge manager knows who the experts are and how to access their knowledge.

Knowledge marshalling

A term used by Colonel Roc Myers[112] to describe the process of gathering knowledge together for a purpose and delivering it to those who need it.

---

[111] Thomas H. Davenport, Thomas H. and Lawrence Prusak, Working Knowledge (Boston. Harvard Business School Press, 1998) p. 5.
[112] Myers, Roc. Strategic Knowledgecraft: Operational Art for the Twenty-First Century. Sept, 2002. http://www.pirp.harvard.edu/pubs_pdf/myers

Learning Organization

A term developed and popularized by Peter Senge and widely used in the knowledge management world to emphasize that an organization needs to have learning imbued into its culture. Learning should be centered on performance and done in the workplace – not through training that takes people away from work into a class.

Manufacturing Age

The era when factories brought people together to do work which was once done at home or in small shops. By bringing workers into an urbanized environment, great efficiencies were gained by controlling and disciplining the workplace and dividing the labor. Work, in a factory before industrialization (when machinery began to change the nature of work), was still done in the same way as before, only now under the discipline of a foreman.

Praxis (Practice)

Germans use "praxis" for the "business" lawyers and doctors maintain; it comprehends all their clients and all the work they do for their clients. Praxis includes more than the English verb to practice; it includes customs and cultural content, as well. Praxis is often translated as "practice" in English, but it comes with very different overtones. Praxis implies a combination of theory and action.

Psyche

Psyche is the Greek word that means both soul and butterfly, alluding to the difficulty of pinning down an exact definition. Not daunted by this difficulty, though, in the early parts of the last century the science of psychology built on this root. We take psychology to mean the study of what makes humans tick. The psyche, then, is the essence of humankind – the what-makes-us-tick stuff.

Self

The Self, when written with a capital "S", is what Jung meant by the new center of the personality after one has undergone the process of individuation, the hero's journey.

Shadow

Those parts of the personality of which we are unaware because there is no "light" cast on them (they dwell in the shadow, unseen). They are usually projected onto others and we can first begin to recognize them by the intensity of our reaction to another's behavior.

Systems thinking

A methodology developed by systems theorists that emphasizes the importance of looking at actions within their context, rather than isolated activities.

Transformation

Transformation is a change that is profound enough to cause a change in the physical, mental, or cultural form of the object or institution.

Work

Work is Force times Distance. It is production, not just activity. Work focuses on those activities that lead to an organization accomplishing its mission. Work is organized through tasks that are linked together in an application – a set of related work activities.

Work culture

Work Culture is the environment in which work is done. It encompasses the attitudes, beliefs and presuppositions that we bring to our work.

Work culture transformation

A transformation of the work culture is evidenced by observed and qualitatively measurable change in behavior – from an information-hoarding to an information-sharing environment.

Workflow

The sequence of tasks, or necessary steps that comprises a business process. Two groups may perform the same work, but use entirely different work processes or workflow. Optimizing workflow removes non-value-added tasks from the work process in order to improve productivity.

Work process

Work processes are comprised of a series of tasks to deliver value to a customer. It is not a department (e.g., Accounts Receivable), nor is it simply a collection of activities or tasks. The tasks must be held together by a mission: delivering value to a customer.

APPENDIX III

Why We Don't Share Information

An Essay

By Noel Dickover

This essay and other creative ideas about work culture, communities of practice, training, and performance can be found at http://www.communibuild.com

What We Learn From Grade School

Roger Shank, a proponent of natural learning theory, claims that real learning slows down when children enter grade school. Before then, learning primarily comes from doing things and being actively involved in the learning process. Children tend to learn best that in which they are interested. There are children who know all 100+ types of Pokeman creatures, but still struggle with learning and remembering the letters of the alphabet.

When they go to grade school, learning becomes disconnected from active participation. Learning becomes an independent chore on which they are graded. Learning becomes stressful, as it is a source of potential disappointment from parents and teachers. Over time, children learn that to become "good students," they must always pay attention even when not interested, and must perform well on the tests and assignments. Evening play-time is taken up with homework assignments that must be completed or bad things will occur.

Eventually children, now called students, learn how to "game" tests. Even though students know they are supposed to really "learn the material," they not graded on how well they actually learn the material, but are graded on how well they perform on the activities and tests. There are many strategies employed. Methods like guessing "C" on multiple choice exams go hand in hand with cramming and other pre-test rituals. Over time, learning becomes more incidental rather than the main task, which is surviving and perhaps excelling at each grade level.

The mortal sin of all schooling, of course, is cheating. Cheating implies you have attempted to shortcut your learning by reading off of someone else's work to get the answer or to figure out how to do something. In the business world we call this activity by other names: knowledge sharing, leveraging expertise, bench-marking, mentoring, etc. Its no wonder people are motivated to hoard knowledge. In school we learn the lesson clearly "Guard your work! Don't let others copy from you!"

This lesson is reinforced in college. You get expelled from college for plagiarizing. The lesson clearly is that students, if they "follow the rules," should do their work independently of others. Only on very specific occasions, often referred to as "group projects," are students allowed to collaborate. Usually, students find group projects to be both stressful and tiring. Group projects involve the students, determining a method for dividing up the tasks into individual chunks for each person to complete. Anger most often accompanies these group projects, as everyone is concerned that the others "won't produce." Students are truly annoyed that their grade is affected by another's performance.

In looking at our education process, it's clear that over time our self worth becomes coupled with what we individually produce. We are incentivized to compete to be the best individual in the group. While we think its "nice" if Sally helps Joey out on a project, Sally is graded only on what she produces. The best of the best of all students are selected to attend the best universities, where they are trained how individually to compete with others like them. The best will go on to get Ph.D.s only after they have successfully "defended" their dissertation of original thought. This is competition at its finest.

Only turn in work when complete!

We are also told time and again to "turn in work when complete." Students are marked down for turning in incomplete assignments. Until complete, work is supposed to be hidden from view. We are allowed to ask questions about our work while preparing it, but are only supposed to present it to others after it is finished. Procrastination, fear of failure, and low self-worth often accompany the turning in of an assignment.

In the business world, the pace of change and communication is such that it is essential to know of problems as soon as they occur and to continually be aware of the direction our collaborators are taking in building products and ideas. There is no better way to do this than by providing the collaborators access to our working files. This notion of sharing the current status on what we are working provides immediate and important feedback to all concerned.

Yet, we often wonder why there is such a cultural barrier to providing access to the working files. While numerous collaboration products are geared around this very notion, few are well employed. Instead we spend immense resources in developing detailed, periodic reports that we "only show when complete." These reports span the gamut of all essential information, including financial health, technical status, organizational and personnel concerns. Until we see the reports, we don't get to know the potential problems, concerns, etc. We do not have key, updated information automatically available at the moment of need.

The Bottom Line

All told, in asking individuals and organizations to move from an information hoarding culture to an information sharing culture, we are really asking people to start interacting in ways they have never previously done. Worse than that, we are asking them to interact in ways that they look down upon as inherently wrong. Our rationale for asking is that making these changes in the workplace leads to a more productive, rewarding environment. Unfortunately, the price of admission for the individual is "giving up" that which drives his/her identity and self worth. We are asking each person not only to provide everything they produce to others, we are asking them to do this before its even complete!

What We Learn from Sports: Notions of Management

Business professionals continually use sports analogies as a way of getting the organization motivated and aligned. Why is this?

Could it be that sports are the only approved place in our educational system in which true teaming is both necessary and encouraged? Well, I suppose both drama and orchestra encourage teamwork, but neither is very sexy or competitive. After all, we all remember the star quarterback from our high school days, but very few ever knew the first chair violinist!

In sports, teamwork is required. The players must work together for the common good. The common good is of course defined as victory, in which successful teams cause other (unsuccessful) teams to lose. Players are told to sacrifice for the needs of the team – this is what is known as being a "team player."

Unfortunately, in sports, the "team players" are directed by the all-powerful and all-knowing coach. It's the coach who sets the pace of operations; the coach who sets the game plan; the coach who sets the mission and end-state; and the coach who makes the corrections. Team players are expected to follow the coach's guidance to the letter.

Is this where we get our traditional notions of management from? In our learning process, we are always looking for models to guide our actions – successful sports coaches are clearly seen as the model representation of excellent managers. One only needs to see the corporate interest in a Pat Riley or Joe Gibbs seminar, or the management books written by coaches, or the famous quotes from coaches like Vince Lombardi ("Winning isn't everything, it's the only thing") tied to both companies and motivational posters.

This dichotomy, most recently found in sports, is not a recent phenomenon. We see it throughout western civilization, in everywhere from God (the shepherd) and his flock, king and country, conquerors and conquered, and Descartes' theoretical Mind and Body separation, to the "Head of household" field on our tax returns. In all these cases it is critical for the "director" to "know" the answer.

What are the cultural implications of viewing management as a sports coach does? Is it any wonder why managers intuitively want to be seen as the "one who knows?" But does today's work environment really lend itself to this dichotomy of those who direct versus those who do?

Why Manager's Hoard Knowledge

Generally, the communication- and information-flows within a work unit are very hierarchical in nature. Members of the work unit are often seen as "collectors of information" that is to be sent to the "one who makes the tough call." The manager may request each subordinate to gather additional information, but the manager is prided on having the "big picture" necessary to make the tough decision. In larger organizations, many employees have no idea what occurs outside of their purview, and often may not even know what is occurring within their work unit. Is it any wonder that managers are paid for making the tough decisions?

Managers often feel the need to protect knowledge in their quest to maintain power and authority. Managers tend to hoard a lot of the information that makes up the "big picture." This means that operational information, financial information, marketing information and technical information are often subject to censure. The manager will attend higher level meetings, and then will disseminate only that portion he/she feels is relevant for the subordinates to know. Subordinates, by definition of their place in the hierarchy, are incapable of making "strategic" judgments in the course of their work.

Unlike a sports team, today's work environment is far from clear or knowable. Most situations pose a bizarre mix of social, political and technical issues that are often jumbled together in strange ways. Managers are continually posed with situations where the problems are unfocussed and the options are unclear. There is no clear solution to most situations. The best we can hope for is enlightened approaches that are continually re-evaluated. Managers who see their job as tied to "knowing" invariably began to exhibit defensive routines when posed with these situations. Their actions become more focused on maintaining power and authority than devising enlightened approaches. Often we refer to this state as "maintaining the status quo."

Middle management and knowledge sharing

Middle management is seen as performing two essential functions:

1 Serve as a communication mechanism up and down the "line;"
2 Make the decisions that affect performance at the appropriate work level.

Middle management prides itself on doing both of these functions successfully. So successfully in fact that middle management is usually seen as the hardest, most entrenched, most difficult group to affect in any organizational change initiative. They have the most to lose in any restructuring, and no longer have unique skill sets from which to gauge their self worth.

Yet, both of these functions are significantly diminished when new technologies are successfully implemented. Communication options have become far more widespread. Information can be automatically collected, combined, attenuated and packaged for both senior management and the rest of the workforce. The potential for making "flat" organizations is greater then ever.

Unfortunately, the communications tools themselves do not lead to improvements in performance without buy-in and support from the members of the organization. Often the improvements result in less of a need for middle management. There is little reason for middle managers to support such efforts if they result in job loss. Middle managers, when presented organizational change options will often go to their roots – hoarding information.

The Bottom Line

The metaphor of "a manager as sports coach" is very detrimental to cultivating a knowledge-sharing environment. Especially large organizations are characterized by having a myriad of communication problems. Often each level of management will hoard essential knowledge that is not delivered "down the pipe." Often the goals themselves are unclear to the average employee. One needs only see the laughter surrounding a Dilbert skit for verification of this sentiment.

Where Do We Go From Here?

This essay, if anything, should impart the folly in thinking that transforming the work culture from an information hoarding environment to an information sharing environment (sometimes referred to as an integrated digital environment) is either easy or driven by technological solutions. Our real culture does not lend itself to sharing. In its best, the vision of our culture is based on rugged individuality. John Wayne and the Marlboro Man are some of our most enduring icons to the rest of the world. It is a culture that has George Washington as the "Father of our country," that honors JP Morgan and Bill Gates, one in which we all want to "be like Mike." Our national anthem is sung not by the masses in a choir setting, its sung individually by our best singers. While rugged individualism provides the fundamental ingredient for our well-renown excellence and innovation, it does not aid our efforts collaborating and sharing.

Although it is not easy, we know it is possible to create knowledge sharing environments. Most of us remember magical times when knowledge sharing has worked, if even for brief periods. To cultivate knowledge sharing cultures, we know at least some of the ingredients required:

Trust: In a trusting environment, work is performed in a transparent environment. The manager trusts that the information used by the subordinate (which is available to the manager at all times) is the latest and most accurate available. The subordinate trusts that his/her data/information are accepted as authoritative and that mistakes that appear in this transparent work environment will be probed and questioned, but not used as a weapon against the worker.

Cooperation: To perform in a knowledge sharing environment, immediate access to information needed to do work requires collaborative relationships, in which each person with a need to know has access to another's work without the owner having to post his/her work and without the seeker gaining access via special permissions. This is a different definition of cooperation and sharing than most are used to – knowledge sharing does not mean "ask me and I'll give it to you," it means I have access without having to ask.

Cultivating a Corporate Memory: A corporate memory allows the knowledge to move from being individually owned and managed to becoming individually owned but organizationally managed. The ownership of the information itself remains tied to the individual or work team that originated it. This allows it to keep its timeliness context and rationale for creation – all of which are essential to understanding why the information is useful. To be effective, this must be a voluntary process, one in which people actually want to participate. Only voluntary participation will yield the best people have to offer – only then will you get access to what people believe to be synonymous with their self-worth. Then, the corporate memory, which is the product of the trusting, cooperative environment, becomes the engine for future innovation.

To be effective, these ingredients need to be artfully crafted over time to form the basis of a knowledge sharing culture. To do so, many skills are required. And while painful and time consuming, if successful, we will have created a magical environment that is a delight to work in, while also being an incredibly powerful organizational performance enhancer.

APPENDIX IV

Integrated Digital Environment

From Ken Megill's Thinking for a Living, Chapter 5

An integrated digital environment is one in which there is immediate access to information needed to do work.

While automation in general and an integrated digital environment in specific are critical to the knowledge worker in the Age of Knowledge, effective automation is about more than wires and computers . . . it is about how we do work. An integrated digital environment is about real people doing real work. An integrated digital environment is exactly that, an environment. It describes the atmosphere, the conditions, the culture, and the "stuff" that makes possible a new way of working – working as knowledge creators. The adjectives that describe that environment, "integrated" and "digital" mean that there are wires and computers, that's the digital part. Integrated describes the ubiquitous connectivity that allows the worker access to all the information needed in order to do real work.

The term "integrated digital environment" is not as widely used as "knowledge work" and "community of practice" in knowledge management discussions. But it is part of the language of information technology. In the IT world, IDE is the term used to describe the technological (generally understood as the hardware, software and connectivity tools) of an organization or an enterprise.

Depending on the focus, each of the terms "Integrated." "digital," and "environment" can become the most important.

- "Digital" refers to the technology that enables knowledge work. It is about the wires and computers that are the tools of the knowledge

trade. It includes the connectivity that enables collaborative work to be done.
- "Environment" refers to the surroundings, to all of the background that makes knowledge work viable. The terms "digital" and "integrated" both modify "environment." A digital environment is contrasted with an analog environment. A digital environment is the world of computers and people who are connected together as a community does its work.
- The "integration" of a digital environment comes through web technology – through linking together communities of practice and disparate individuals and groups within an organization. The web came possible when people adopted protocols – standards – for communication. These standards create an environment in which information sharing is the norm. A new world of discourse arose.

The initials IDE were initially used to refer to "integrated data environment" – a technical environment in which databases could be integrated, generally by intermediate data bases (or middle ware) that enables databases created for disparate situations to be accessible from a single source.

The integration in a digital environment increases the possibility for knowledge work to become the norm, not the exception. Through the adoption and use of communication standards, open architectures, increased communication capabilities and agreements to share appropriate information among business units and throughout industries a new environment necessary for knowledge work is created. This environment includes technologies, but more importantly, it includes ways of working that emphasize and enable information sharing.

The term integrated digital environment in the United States government was popularized by former Vice president Albert Gore as a part of the reinvention of government movement to refer to the technical environment necessary for a new way to do government business.

The Department of Defense has had a formally constituted program for several years to develop an integrated digital environment and the term is widely used. Each of the Services, as is normally the case, uses the term in different ways and there is no agreement on what the term means.

For some, an integrated digital environment is identical with an integrated data environment – an environment in which data can be shared among various agencies, among contractors and the government, and among businesses within an industry. In the industrial world it often refers to ways in which different businesses, both within the same company and among various companies, can share data and information using a common language or database.

For others, however, the phrase takes on a more robust meaning. In the US Air Force the focus in the integrated digital environment project quickly moved beyond developing wires and computers to a new way of doing business. In this chapter we shall use the term "integrated digital environment" to mean an environment in which the information needed to do business is immediately accessible. This is the definition adopted by the Air Force project and being used by a Work Culture Transformation Board established to implement the conclusions of that project.

APPENDIX V

A Work Culture Transformation Assessment

In which we share with the readers an instrument we developed and tested for measuring transformation in the work culture – and we invite feedback.

ABOUT A WORK CULTURE TRANSFORMATION ASSESSMENT

A Work Culture Transformation Assessment is an instrument that was created by the Work Culture Transformation Board Staff to provide an instrument to measure change in the work culture. It is an instrument that is still in its testing phase and the author invites comment and input as others use the tool.

The assessment is a three-stage process; it involves a collection of people's stories about their experience with the work culture transformation, observations by a trained observer, and a questionnaire that addresses trust, cooperation, and the preservation of knowledge. The assessment process involves a week of observations and conversations with people in the work site, initial meetings with the leadership, out-briefings with the same leaders and responses to the questionnaire by a sample of leaders and work force.

Observation

Observation is an on-going process during the week in which a trained observer assesses and notes the work atmosphere: how do people relate to each other? Is work being done? Are people too busy to be helpful or informative? Is the pace frenetic? Are people watching the clock to tell when quitting time arrives? As people open their e-mails, does a din of groans ensue? Do people know where to find the tools they need to do their work?

Stories

People's stories emerge in formal and informal settings, sometimes over lunch or coffee, sometimes in interviews, sometimes as responses to an invitation on the questionnaire to share their vision of a transformed work culture and to provide input into the qualities that an assessment of the work culture should address.

Questionnaire

The sample of respondents to the questionnaire is chosen in collaboration with the leadership at the organization. When the leadership and the assessor have reached agreement about who should receive the questionnaire, an e-mail giving the URL where the questionnaire can be found is sent to the potential respondents. They are asked if they would please take 5 to 10 minutes to respond to the questions by the close of business the second day.

Review Process

The assessor/observer collects the responses and reviews the observations, stories and responses to questions. Any gaps in the information can be identified at that time and corrected on the fourth day. The final day is spent in out-briefings with the leadership.

Qualitative measures

The work culture in its most important aspects is not quantifiable; it is made up of the attitudes, beliefs and presuppositions people bring to their work. As Albert Einstein reminds us, "All that can be counted does not count and all that counts cannot be counted."

EXAMPLE: RESULTS OF AN ASSESSMENT AT ONE ORGANIZATION

In which the results in one organization are summarized

Observations

The work environment is an open, friendly, welcoming one. The atmosphere gives an appearance of calm industry, people doing serious work without the air of frenzy and chaos prevalent in many workplaces. During the assessment, people were gracious in taking time for answering questions, providing helpful comments. They were eager to talk about their work and its transformation. They were thoughtful in their answers and forthcoming in their views of both the positive and negative aspects of the transformation. Their vision of what is possible with the transformation seems clear and often very exciting. Many people, in describing their vision of the perfect information-sharing world, state that their work environment in this organization provides their ideal.

Stories

Three types of stories emerged during conversations and from comments on the questionnaire. We'll characterize them as Pride of Ownership, Frustration with "Covered Wagon" State of the Web, and Visions of the Possible.

Pride of Ownership

> *The stories that portrayed the pride of ownership felt by the people whose work was accessed and relied upon by the leadership were the most striking because of their frequency and the excitement they conveyed. The fact that leaders were interested in their work, viewed it in-process, commented on it occasionally, and counted on its accuracy and timeliness elevated the status of worker to knowledge worker. One person who worked previously in an office that did business "the old way," as he called it, commented on how excited he was by the concept of the creator is the owner and is responsible and accountable for his creation. His frustration lay in the fact that it took some months before he knew how to do this. He needed training that was "just in time and just for him" – training that was integral to the work processes.*

Frustration with "Covered Wagon" State of the Web

Many people spoke of their frustration with the current state of the art as it exists at this organization. One person reported that the Organization's web site was the largest on the East Coast but the access to it among the least reliable. This provides the rationale for a continued reliance on the shared hard-drive for doing work: "At least it never 'goes down.'" When work is not done on the web, but posted to the web after being completed on the shared drive, the trust in the currency of information on the web is lacking. Still others lamented that there was no common lexicon, no guidelines for what is posted, or how it is posted. There was also very little confidence that either quality control or technological reviews were done on any regular basis or with any consistency.

Visions of the Possible

There was an infectious optimism palpable in the atmosphere of meetings where access has replaced reporting – meeting agenda and content was accessed on the web and projected where all could see. People spoke of their visions for the workplace when the technology has reached its most reliable state and when other work cultures with which they interface have also undertaken the transformation to an integrated digital environment. Some of the direct comments in this area speak more eloquently than a summary of them. They can be viewed in the sections called Culture Change and Visions at the end of this assessment.

The Questionnaire

The questionnaire addressed people's perceptions of the work culture in three areas: Trust, Cooperation, and Preservation of Knowledge

Trust

The questions in the trust section were designed to elicit perceptions about whether leaders and co-workers use and value their work. Our assumption is that until others access the information/knowledge and make use of it as is (i.e. trust that it is of value), the environment is not a safe one in which to make one's work available. Before people are willing to share information and work in a transparent work environment, they must trust that the information they create will be used in the spirit in which it was created and that there will be no negative consequences from their having made work, ideas and creations accessible. In this organization slightly more than half of the respondents said they believed that the work culture promoted trust. Their comments at the end of the assessment detail insightful comments on the meaning of trust and its implications in the workplace.

Leadership and staff alike stated many times and in many ways their perception that real change is led from the top and accomplished from the bottom and that leadership is "90 percent example." Without strong, enthusiastic, articulate leadership:

- setting the example,
- educating,
- advocating,
- rewarding, and
- supporting people to "go and do likewise,"

people (naturally risk averse) will maintain their comfortable, safe, known ways of doing things; most will not venture forth into unknown territory.

Cooperation

The questions on cooperation were designed to elicit information on the extent to which people share rather than hoard information. The first question addressed the sharing of work products. There was an almost unanimous perception that such information is shared. However, when it is a question of more subtle and traditionally held-close-to-the-chest information, there was a heavier weighting toward the occasionally/never end of the spectrum.

Preservation of Knowledge

This section of questions was designed to elicit perceptions of how easy it is to access stored knowledge; how dependable stored knowledge is – whether it was created yesterday or three years ago. Responses in this section of the questionnaire reflect and provide insight into the frustrations people experience with the technology and work processes of preserving knowledge for reuse (the corporate memory).

Selected meanings of Culture Change submitted by respondents

What follows are selected comments in response to the invitation at the beginning of the questionnaire: "So that we can understand your framework, please tell us what culture change, particularly as it pertains to work, means to you." The only edit has been to eliminate redundancy.

- Tangible differences in the way we do business.
- A new way of thinking about the way in which we conduct our daily business.
- Breaking down stovepipes and doing things differently when traditional processes and practices are no longer effective or efficient.
- Culture change is about attitude, education and acceptance. It means learning about others and their roles/missions and understanding their point of view. It is learning, tolerating and accommodating the opinions of others even when it does not meet or coincide with your own perceived goals/objectives or the central theme.
- Culture change means the organization's values and norms change. This can occur only when actively supported and demonstrated by the senior leadership in the organization.
- Cultural change in the workplace means incorporating new ways of doing business functions. This includes new process steps, new technology and new thinking. Cultural change means we are changing a traditional way of doing activity. It requires commitment, dedication, and enthusiasm. Leadership must not only endorse the change, but also actively communicate the change and participate in the change. Leadership must also be attuned to listening for feedback – it is rare to get everything right the first time.

Visions of the perfect integrated digital environment

What follows are selected comments from the questionnaire in response to the invitation to "Describe your vision of the perfect world of an electronic information sharing environment." The only edit has been to eliminate redundancy.

- A search engine that reads your mind.
- An easy-to-navigate web.
- Ready access to useful materials with one identifier and one password.
- Someone to filter through the "garbage" not of interest to the current user.
- Accurate, timely information available when needed.
- Never having to create another piece of paper from the "ground" up.
- A portal-type environment where everything is in one place, stored in logical fashion and everyone has access to the same information.
- One document, one place, tell me where it is, don't send it to me. If you think anyone can benefit, make it available/accessible on the web.
- The availability/access to sufficient information sources to acquire needed/wanted information to understand and/or conduct the organization's business:
  - data generated once and used for multiple applications, easily accessible.
  - automated way to store and retrieve documents – summary information easy to search.
- A world where the "change" and tool:
  1 Meets the requirement (don't need a baseball bat to squash a mosquito).
  2 Is planned in advanced.
  3 Is technologically correct, and not obsolete at the time of execution
  4 Is executed on a posted schedule.
  5 Users are trained properly.

Roadblocks to creating the perfect world today

What follows are comments gathered in conversation as well as culled from various parts of the questionnaire.

Technical impediments

- Inadequate bandwidth during peak hours deters the sharing of information.
- Unreliability of the web. Many commented that they did their work on the shared drive because it, unlike the web, was always available. If they need to do work and the web is down, it causes delays. It may also account for a general lack of trust that what is posted to the web is the latest, most accurate information.

- Systems that are set up for people who sit at their desks with a high speed LAN connection. "When on travel, I must rely on a 12000 BPS modem connection; a 1-MB brief is painfully slow to download. There needs to be either a faster way to connect or web pages must be made leaner."
- Lack of a common language and standards for information databases and a common process for storing and making available information. There is also a lack of a common method for assessing the value of information. The analogy would be that the whole world speaks, writes, and understands one language.
- Overwhelming volume of e-mail; we can't read them all. We could easily spend all day just reading and answering e-mail.
- Lack of training on how to store information and keep it current. (Database that is 80% correct is not really worth keeping.)

Cultural impediments

Many comments came in this category:

- The web diminishes human contact, so one's work becomes drier and less interesting.
- Different types of personalities respond to different types of rewards: some respond to praise, some to the symbols of power (money, status), some to recognition of their competence, some to recognition of their creativity, etc. We haven't discovered yet how to give web-rewards. A poignant example of this, "I do not care how significant of insignificant my part of the whole is, I care that my part is understood and recognized by those who participate in management and decision-making forums."
- Allowing people to "dress down" and telecommute as much as possible would empower our people with the trust, belief, and tools to do our job.

Incomplete information:

- The often-unconscious clues one gets from body language about another's trustworthiness are not available on the web, or even via video conferencing. This means one is making decisions about trusting someone with partial information.
- Need for uniform corporate definitions.
- Training needed in all areas.

- "Retrieval is miserable, which means even if the information is out there, I can't get it." Similarly: "The greatest curse is 'It's on the Web.' People forget to say where and forget to notify when things change."
- The trend is for the leadership to have more access to details that weren't readily available to them before. That leads to micromanagement, which is needed in some cases but fuels a stronger desire for detail from micro-managers. We expect answers and information "at the speed of light," which isn't always possible or may result in less than accurate information.
- There are adversarial relationships where there don't need to be. Also, we receive taskings for the same information in different formats from several "higher headquarters." These headquarters elements apparently do not pool their information (i.e., cooperate) and usually require enough difference in format to cause a rework of the information.

Select comments on trust:

What follows are the selected comments of those who responded to the invitation to add other elements of trust to the assessment instrument. The only edit has been to eliminate redundancy.

- Do you make personal contact with the people who supply you information electronically to put faces with names?
- As a decision-maker, how often do you reach your decision based on the information supplied you by the creator(s)?
- Do you get the information you need when you access the information created by co-workers?
- Do existing processes and permissions facilitate the flow of information?
- Does your Integrated Digital Environment provide you the information you need about the creator and currency of the information on which you must rely?
- Have you ever been "burned" by sharing information?
- Do information-creators trust what will happen with their work products when in the hands of peers and/or decision makers (interpreted fairly, credit given where credit is due, etc.)?
- What happens when something goes wrong? How will you be informed something is wrong?

Selected comments on Cooperation:

What follows are the selected comments from questionnaire respondents on what other elements of cooperation might be included in the assessment. The only edit has been to eliminate redundancy.

- Are the lessons you learn in the process of performing specific tasks automatically captured and made available to others?
- Do people willingly seek out other relevant knowledge?
- Do people who have the relevant knowledge willingly share it with others?
- Might also address active mentoring roles as sign of willingness to pass along that which will make others successful. The "Good Ol' Boy" network is far from dead and Golden Children with little talent still manage to succeed.
- Are you openly recruiting ideas and not forcing solutions on people?
- Do you have the tools to cooperate?

Selected comments on the preservation of knowledge for reuse:

What follows are selected comments from respondents to the invitation to add other elements to the assessment instrument in the field of knowledge preservation. The only edit has been to eliminate redundancy.

- Does your information system capture the date and time the information was last updated?
- Does your information system capture how many people view it?
- Have people been trained to put out web-based information and access?
- Is the web-based information accessible if you are not at the same location? (E.g., server issues, security codes, travel).
- Does the organization have an organizational plan for knowledge management?
- Is there a clear understanding of how information is to be stored and organized? (The method itself, how to recreate the task that someone has passed along.)

APPENDIX VI

A Workbook for Transformation

Paving the way for transformation

The questions in this workbook are designed to help leaders and communities of practice get started in their thinking, planning, and brainstorming about the kinds of changes involved in organizational transformation.

I. What is the organization's mission?

II. What are the mission-essential tasks of the organization?

III. How will the work involved in performing the above mission-essential tasks change with the transition to an integrated digital environment?

1   How is collective knowledge and information made available when the worker needs it?

2   How do we create an idiot-proof, intuitively-obvious, easily-accessible site on which the worker looks for essential information?

- Collaborative workspace technology
  - How easy is it to access?
  - How reliable is it?
  - How user-friendly is it?
- Rewards for collaboration/consequences for "going it alone"
  - How are workers rewarded – what are the carrots?
  - What are the sticks?

3   Has the organization assured that creative, non-linear thinkers are attracted to the work pool?

4   How does the worker get quick feedback needed in the "tight spiral" environment of e-revolution?

5   Does the organization attract and reward creative "edge of the community" workers who can develop technology quickly?

6   How does the organization support the creation of communities of interest?

7   Does the organization support communication between communities?

8   Is the organization retraining, encouraging and rewarding managers to become facilitators?

9   Is the organization encouraging and rewarding flexibility of work assignments?

10 How are the accuracy, timeliness, and reliability of the workers' work rewarded and what are the consequences for slow, inaccurate, unreliable work?

- What are the carrots?
- What are the sticks?
- Can and do managers and supervisors trust the workers' work?

11 Do the "standards" reflect rigidity about *what* must be done and flexibility about *how* it gets done?

12 How has the ease and reliability of connectivity between communities been guaranteed?

13 Has the decision-making been shifted to the community doing the work?

14 Is the organization encouraging and rewarding the connectivity between the "needers" of products and services and the "suppliers" of products and services?

Index

action on the journey 115–117
  bows and arrows 109
  creativity 15, 21, 49n, 115–116, 121, 128n
  curiosity 143 148, 149
  focus 87, 116–117
  swords 109–110, 120, 132, 141
  horses, teams of 22, 109, 117
adventure 14, 22, 29–34
  adventurers 14, 114, 121
  beginning the 4–56
  change as 22, 80
  growing up as 40
  love of 14
  sense/spirit of 31, 32
  See also call
Ages
  Stone 5
  Bronze 5
  Dark 47
  Discovery 4
  Agrarian 5, 23
  Manufacturing 5, 156, 157
  Industrial 5, 155
    characteristics of 21, 101, 105
    culture of 17–18, 94, 97, 100
    change from Agrarian to 23
  Information 4, 5, 20–21, 156
  Knowledge 156

assessing the transformation to 183–186
automation in 169–171
culture of 5, 7–24, 30, 83–84, 90
leadership for 32, 109–117
transformation into 5, 16–18, 20–23, 50–51
aid, from unexpected places 53, 59, 64, 120
  See also help
alchemist/alchemy 103
ally 113–114
analytical psychology *See* psychology, analytical
anima 88, 153
animus 39, 88, 153
anthropology/anthropologists 9–10
Arab Human Development Report, 2002 10, 12–13
archetype 38–39
Argonauts 114, 146–147
armo 110–114, 117, 120
Assessment, Work Culture Transformation 173–174, 175–182
  See also questionnaire
astrology 3
attitudes for the journey 109–117

188   Index

Ruth, George Herman ("Babe")   26
B.P.R.   See business process re-engineering
ba   153
baby, the   86, 99
   as symbol of work culture transformation   78, 79, 83, 85, 104
baker, the   87, 88, 116
Baobab tree   90
Bateson, Gregory   57
Bateson, Mary Catherine   57, 61
blacksmith, the   88
Blatner, Adam   37n
Bodi tree   90
boon   64, 99, 112, 120–121
   as a stage of transformation   53, 61–62, 111
   in particular tales   40, 84–85, 104, 111, 117
   in psychodramatic enactment   134–135
   refusing to return with   44, 66
   transformed work culture as   51
boss, the   39, 59, 84, 94, 131
Brooks, David   64n
Buddha   90
bum, the   88
business process reengineering   51

Campbell, Joseph   26–27, 29, 36, 41–44, 53–54, 56, 66–67
candlestick-maker, the   87, 89, 116
call to adventure, the   57, 126–127
   accepting   38, 44, 117
   as a stage of transformation   53, 54–56
   attitudes toward   24, 31, 33–34, 44, 61–62
   in particular tales and stories   40, 55, 56
   in personal life   63–64
   in the workplace   26, 64–66, 119–120, 129, 134, 162
   refusing   22n, 43, 44, 56, 58, 66–67
   trust and   112
CEO   See Chief Executive Officer
change   13, 29, 111
   agents   115, 132
   and the culture   17, 48, 51
   call to   34, 49, 64, 67
   from frog to prince   14, 23, 46, 66, 109–110, 113, 144–145
   in the workplace   22–23, 66–67, 125–137, 165–166, 173–186

management   11, 121
psychological   42–44
in attitude.   See attitudes for the journey
in technology   126, 138
See also transformation
Chief Executive Officer (CEO)   48, 94, 114, 130
Clinton, William Jefferson (Bill)   117
collaboration   5, 11, 14, 19, 87, 163, 184
Cole, Johnetta   60, 61
Columbus, Christopher   4, 56, 110, 121, 129
common sense   10, 11, 17, 20, 23
community   38, 87–91, 154, 184
   as agent of transformation   11–12, 79, 83–85, 96–98, 101, 114–116, 126–127
   as armor   117
   as hero   14, 67, 87, 90, 120
   as recipient of the boon   61, 64, 66
   as source of creativity   116
   digital environment and   170
   in psychological development   88
   in Rumpelstiltskin   14, 15, 89
   of practice   19, 78–79, 86, 105, 122–123, 131–134, 154
   pre-war, a   91
   scientific   18
   network   21
computer   11, 16, 17, 18
consultant   58, 74, 79, 86, 100, 130, 134
cooperation   87n, 155, 167, 173, 176, 177, 182
cosmic two-by-four   See two-by-four
creativity   15, 21, 39, 49n, 59
   See also creativity under action for the journey
Cupid   See Eros
cyclops   57, 110

data   20, 103, 154, 155, 170
Davenport, Thomas H.   155–156
Davies, Robertson   3
death   4, 43n, 145–146
   as initiator of a call to adventure   55, 61, 119
   near-death experience   47, 48, 63
   of the Industrial Age   100
development   10, 12–13, 49n, 121
Diaghilev, Serge   91
Dickover, Noel   20, 161
discovering a name   See naming

ditch-digger 16–17, 22
dungeon 73, 78, 84, 102, 104
DuPont, Alfred I. 57, 61
dwarf 57, 59, 83, 84–85, 86, 99, 101
　See also Rumpelstiltskin

ego 38, 42, 88, 94, 97, 100, 102, 104, 154
elephant, twelve blindfolded men and the 108
Empire, Holy Roman 47
entrepreneur 97
Eros 55, 59, 111, 116, 148
eye, third See third eye
evidence, essential 12

fairy tales/myths
　Arthur (King) and Excalibur 26, 115, 141
　Beauty and the Beast 14, 57, 111, 142
　Bluebeard 117, 143
　Cinderella 55, 112, 119, 143–144
　Fisherman and his Wife 15, 113, 144
　Frog King, The 48, 55, 59, 144–145
　Hansel and Gretel 15, 39, 40, 61, 114, 119, 145
　Inanna 82, 113, 145–146
　Jack and the Beanstalk 14, 55, 59, 112, 117, 146
　Jason and the Golden Fleece 61, 104, 114, 146–147
　Little Red Riding Hood 14, 50, 121, 147
　Psyche 26, 55, 59, 100, 111, 116–117, 119, 148
　Sleeping Beauty 85, 117, 149
　Snow White and the Seven Dwarves 15, 57, 112, 149–150
　Ulysses 14, 26, 57, 114, 119, 137, 150
　See also mythology; myths (for general references to the use of fairy tales and myths)
firefighters, New York 26
first-born 74
Freud, Sigmund 31, 33, 36–37, 41, 91
Frog See Frog King under fairy tales/myths
　See also from frog to prince under change

Gandhi, Mohandas 26
gold/golden 104
　age of myth-making 42
　alchemists and 103
　as something of value 78, 94, 96, 103
　consultants and 79
　in particular tales:
　　Bluebeard 143
　　Cinderella 144
　　Frog King 55, 59, 146–147
　　Jack and the Beanstalk 14, 112, 146
　　Jason and the Golden Fleece 61, 114, 146
　　Moses 129
　　Rumpelstiltskin 67, 73–76, 79, 83–84, 87, 92
　　Psyche 148
　knowledge as 84, 89, 91, 100, 103, 105
　produced by spinning wheel/computer 18, 57, 77, 78, 83, 101, 105
Glennie, Page 13
gnome 78
　See also dwarf and Rumpelstiltskin
greed 15, 86, 93–94, 96, 113
guru 79, 90, 97, 100, 134

Hades 116–117
　See also underworld
"happily-ever-after" 50, 61, 137–138, 150
health care 65
help 30–31, 33–34, 44, 49, 117, 122
　as a stage of transformation 53, 59–60, 64, 80–81, 111
　creativity as 115
　in particular myths/tales:
　　Hansel and Gretel 40
　　Hercules 109
　　Inanna 146
　　King Arthur 115
　　Psyche 100
　　Sleeping Beauty 85
　　psychodramatic enactment 133–135
　　Rumpelstiltskin 84, 97–98, 100–101, 111, 117
　See also aid
Henry, Patrick 65
"here lie monsters." See "hic sunt animales"
Hera 26
Hercules 14, 109, 134, 138, 146
hero/es 25–44, 154

Index 189

as ordinary people 49–50, 56, 60
community as 90
courage of 58
cultural 14, 26–27, 85, 119–121
despair and 80
equipment for 22, 108–117
miller as 92
miller's daughter as 97
psychodrama of 125–135
rest for 137–138
Rumpelstiltskin as 100
See also aid; boon; call to adventure; help; triumph; transformation; specific tales/myths
"hic sunt animales" 4, 44, 121
hoarding 15, 78, 79, 101, 133, 158, 163
  middle managers and 166
  Rumpelstiltskin and 86
Holy Roman Empire See Empire, Holy Roman
Howe, Elias 59–60, 79

IDE See Integrated Digital Environment
individuation 116, 154, 155
information 18–24, 155–156, 169–171
  access to 11–12, 103, 110, 112, 122, 132–135
  Age, See under Ages
  data and 154
  gathered by the community 87–89
  management 155
  salons and 91
  sciences 16
  sharing of 11, 30, 158, 161–167, 175, 178
  Work Culture Transformation Assessment and 173–182
  See also hoarding
initiation, rite of 34, 47
Integrated Digital Environment (IDE) 21, 48, 135, 155, 166, 169–171, 176, 178–181, 183
intuition 21

Jung, Carl 1, 26, 36–44, 49, 88, 91, 116, 141, 157

Keirsey, D. & D.W. 21n
king, the 22, 73–76, 78–79, 83–85, 94–95, 115, 130–131
  and greed 81, 126
  as a modern symbol 86
  In tale of Rumpelstiltskin 15, 73–76, 92–93, 96–104
  particular names of: Minos 58; Gordius 121; of Ithaca 109; Uther Pendragon 141
  See also specific fairy tales/myths
kingdom
  and the journey refused 22n, 99
  animal 4, 9
  in business 89, 99, 130
  in psychological development 88, 94
  in the tale of Rumpelstiltskin 74, 79, 83, 85, 87
knowledge 11, 24, 48, 94, 155, 184
  Age See under Ages
  and culture 9, 20–21
  as a resource 29, 30n
  as armor See armor
  as gold 84, 104
  as power 100–101, 105
  as transforming 4
  creativity and 59
  hoarding 75, 86, 164
  in the workplace 36, 99, 123, 162, 164–167, 169–171
  making/finding 18–19, 51, 83, 103, 153, 155
  management 16, 19, 156–157, 182
  manager 156
  marshalling 156
  preservation of 5, 122–123, 135, 154, 167, 176–182
  sharing 162, 165–167
  technology and 51
  the community and 79–80, 83–85, 88–91, 154
  work 12–13, 19, 20–22, 36, 87n, 169–171
  worker 11, 16–18, 88, 113, 121, 135

labyrinth 29, 58
leader/leadership
  as a sword 115
  equipping the 32–33, 52, 89
  of pre-war cultural elite 91
  of work culture transformation 24, 106, 113, 119–121, 127
  psychological, Self as 88
  refusing the call to adventure 44
  success as a challenge to 48

Index 191

symbols of in *Rumpelstiltskin* 79, 83, 85, 86, 93
training 32, 51, 121
See also Assessment, Work Culture transformation 175–183
learning organization *See* organization, learning

Mandela, Nelson 56, 61
maiden 67, 70, 89
  call to adventure of 84
  in psychodramatic enactment 130–132
  in tale of 73–76
  symbolism of 78–79, 81, 96–98
  workers as 18, 83, 86, 102
  See also miller's daughter
Mann, Thomas 41
management 123, 126, 135, 164–165, 180
  total quality 51
  See also under change; information; knowledge
Manufacturing Age *See under* Ages
map
  Columbus' and his era 4, 44, 110
  for transformation 65, 66, 120–121
  lack of 32, 44, 58, 61, 85
  psychological 32, 82
  stories in stead of 110
markers for the journey 15, 40, 114, 120
martyr 66, 88
Matisse, Henri 41
maiden *See* miller's daughter
Mead, Margaret 57
medicine man *See* shaman
Megill, Kenneth 11–12, 16–17, 19, 87n, 153, 169–171
MBTI *See* Myers Briggs Type Inventory
Miller, James G. 38
miller, the 15, 92–93, 130
miller's daughter 15, 126
  in tale of Rumpelstiltskin 73–76
  symbolism of 96–98
  workers as 84, 86, 103
  See also queen
Minos, King 58
mission
  community's 78, 79, 83, 87–89, 101
  in business 110, 122, 125, 132, 138, 158, 159, 183
  in sports 164

leader and 89
  need for each worker to know 18–19
  psychological 88
  production, mode of 11, 23, 105, 155
monomyth 41–43
  See also mythology
monsters
  in wilderness stage of transformation 33, 53, 56, 62, 111, 120
  inhabiting unknown parts of the earth 22, 112
  help slaying 114, 138
  See also "hic sunt animales"
Moreno, Joseph 1, 35–37, 43–44, 91
Moses 56, 129
Munich 41
Myers Briggs Type Inventory (MBTI) 21
myth
  aid/help in 115
  boon/triumph in 61
  call to adventure in 56, 58
  curiosity in 117
  earliest 113
  embodying heroic attitudes 111
  embodying values 14–16
  in psychology 26n, 34, 41–44, 81, 106
  providing metaphors for transformation 27, 49–50, 54, 77
  See also mythology; specific titles under fairy tales/myths
mythology 99, 115
  See also monomyth; myth; specific titles under fairy tales/myths

name/naming 81, 84, 86, 94, 105
  and Rumpelstiltskin's death 100, 132
  community finds the 14, 83–85, 87, 89, 130
  in the tale of *Rumpelstiltskin* 75–76
New York 26, 36, 61

over-achiever, the 88
Obi-Wan Kanobe 100
organization, learning 135, 157
owner 17, 94, 102, 130, 135, 167, 175

Paine, Thomas 65
palaver 90
paradigm shift 23, 49, 79, 95
Paris 36, 41, 91
Picasso, Pablo 44, 91

Post, Emily 57
practice 157
praxis *See* practice
protagonist 10, 37, 54, 59, 127
psyche 37–41, 60, 82, 88, 92, 106, 153, 157
  See also "Psyche" under fairy tales/myths
psychodrama/psychodramatic 36–37, 43–44, 97, 107–108, 125–135

queen
  and a new culture 78, 99
  as psychological symbol 96–97
  collaborating with the community 78, 79, 87–88, 116, 120
  in other fairy tales/myths 15, 61, 145, 149–150
  in the tale of *Rumpelstiltskin* 74–75
  workers as 77, 83, 86, 99
  See also miller's daughter
questionnaire, Work Culture Transformation Assessment 173–182

Rand McNally 45
reductionism 33–35
revolution 47, 51, 57, 82, 119
  American 61, 65
  Industrial 13, 84, 120, 155
  e-revolution 184
risk-taking 14
road map *See* map
Rumpel *See* Rumpelstiltskin
Rumpelstiltskin
  as helper 59, 70, 84, 105
  as hoarder 86, 96
  as psychological symbol 81
  death of 83
  in the psychodramatic enactment 130–131
  significance today 36, 77–80
  symbol of 100–101
  tale of as hero's journey 84
  See also Rumpelstiltskin (the tale) 73–76

salesman/sales-manager 79, 86, 92
salon, literary and intellectual 91
Schantz, Herb 119
self 38, 42, 154, 157
Senge, Peter 157
sensation 21

shadow 39, 88, 158
shaman 57
sociology/sociologists 9–10
sociometry 37
socius 37
spinning wheel 79, 101, 105, 131
Star Wars 100
straw 77–79, 83, 103, 105, 128
  See also the tale of Rumpelstiltskin, 73–76
systems thinking 158

technology 51, 92
  as an instrument for the call to adventure 65, 79–80, 126, 132, 138
  frustrations of 128, 130, 133
  in the Industrial Age 4, 18, 126
  in an Integrated Digital Environment 169, 176, 177, 178
  providing relief from tedium 20
telecommuting 21
terra incognita 23, 49, 64, 112, 119, 121, 138, 150, 177
Theodorson, George and Achilles 9
thinking 21n, 22, 108, 120, 130, 178
  Thinking for a Living 12n 19n, 84n, 122n, 169
  As an activity of work 21, 97 *See also* ditch diggers
  See also systems thinking
third eye, the 2, 77, 134
threshold 14, 30–31, 55, 58, 73, 114
total quality management (TQM) *See under* management
transformation 4, 23, 158
  experts in 82
  in the tale of Rumpelstiltskin 73, 77–80, 100
  of work 13, 19, 30, 138
  of the hero 26, 29, 36, 109–117
  stages of 45–62
  personal 31–34, 35, 38, 40, 42–43, 63–64
  process of 36, 82, 106
  organizational 22–24, 64–67, 83, 119–123, 125–135
  See also Assessment, Work Culture Transformation
trials 47, 49, 111, 114, 120, 148
triumph 27, 53, 54, 61, 64
  See also boon

trust 112, 166
  as attribute of Knowledge Age 5, 20, 22–23, 134
  as value 14, 30, 89
  views of in a real life workplace 173, 176–177, 179–181
Tutu, Bishop Desmond 23
two-by-four 26, 44, 54, 57, 60, 62, 65, 66, 73, 130, 134
  See also call, the
Tylor, E.B. 9

underworld, the 113, 116–117, 146, 148
See also Hades
unknown territory See terra incognita

values 14–15
  See also *Arab Human Development Report, 2002*
Vienna 36, 91
village square 90
Vikings 121
wandering 53, 56–62, 129–130, 134, 138, 148
  See also wilderness

washerwoman, the 88
Wiesel, Eli 56, 61

wholeness 39–40, 43–44, 96
wilderness
  as a stage of transformation 53, 56–58, 59, 62, 64–66, 120
  in fairy tales/myths 40, 56, 73, 84, 114, 117
  in psychodramatic enactment 129–132, 134, 135
  psychological 44
  See also wandering; terra incognita
Williams, Anthony 37n
wisdom 4, 16, 44, 50, 58, 120
witch 15, 40, 88, 137, 145
World War I 36
Work Culture Transformation Board of the United States Air Force 171, 173
worker 11, 16, 18, 21, 30, 112, 114, 181, 184
  maiden as 79, 86, 97
  See also under knowledge

Yoda 100

Zander, Benjamin and Rosamund Stone 49n
Zen 59, 112–113
Zipes, Jack 43n, 76n

K · G · Saur Verlag

Information Services
Management Series

Guy St. Clair

Beyond Degrees
Professional Learning in the Information Services Environment

2003. xxvi, 315 pages. Hardbound € 88.00. ISBN 3-598-24369-3

Knowledge Services is an enterprise-wide management methodology that enables companies and organizations achieve excellence, both in the performance of internal staff and in their interactions with external customers.

Knowledge Services is more than knowledge management. Defined as the convergence of information management, knowledge management, and strategic (performance-centered) learning, Knowledge Services recognizes that the most critical asset in any group or environment is what its people know. This knowledge - this intellectual capital - is the organization's primary asset, and Knowledge Services is the tool the organization uses for managing this corporate asset.

This book provides the Knowledge Services professional with guidelines for conceptualizing, designing, implementing, and measuring successful programs for professional learning, staff development, and professional growth in the organization, all within the knowledge services framework.

Contents include: Knowledge Services as a New Profession - Professionalism, Accreditation, and Certification - KD/KS: Knowledge Development and Knowledge Sharing - Qualification Management in the New Profession - Managing Strategic Learning Within the Organization.

Sue Henczel

The Information Audit
A Practical Guide

2001. xxiv, 272 pages. Hardbound € 68.00. ISBN 3-598-24367-7

The information audit is a process by which a library or information centre reviews and assesses its holdings, services, etc. This topic is one that has generated much interest over the last few years. The Information Audit: A Practical Guide will take the information professional through the stages of conducting an audit, from planning and carrying out to assessing and presenting the results and how to implement findings.

As an aid to understanding, the book contains four international case studies to illustrate the information audit process in action.

The Information Audit is directed at library managers in all sectors, but particularly those in special libraries, students and lecturers in library and information science.

Contents include: The changing role of the corporate information unit; Planning the audit; Data collection; Data analysis; Data evaluation; Communicating recommendations; Implementing recommendations; The information audit as a continuum; Summary and case studies.

www.saur.de

Guides to Information Sources

Information Sources in **Art, Art History and Design**
Edited by Simon Ford
2001. XX, 220 pages Hardbound € 98.00. ISBN 3-598-24438-X

Like all sectors of the information profession, art librarianship is undergoing a period of major change. Recognition of the economic importance of the creative industries and the expansion of the further and continuing education sector, has meant an increasing number of people are seeking information on art, art history and design. The pressure to connect these people with multiplying fields of knowledge, accessible through an ever increasing variety of formats, has led to innovative new forms of service delivery.

Information Sources in Art, Art History and Design reviews current practice from a variety of perspectives, drawing on the subject knowledge of specialists based in the UK, USA and the Netherlands. Each chapter provides a guide to the best sources of information on a range of subjects, including "General reference sources", "The art book", "Auction catalogues" and "Multicultural art and design".

Information Sources in Art, Art History and Design is a welcome addition to the Guide to Information Sources series. It is edited by Simon Ford, Special Collections Bibliographer at the National Art Library, Victoria and Albert Museum, and written by experts who evaluate the best sources in their field.

Information Sources in **Music**
Edited by Lewis Foreman
2003. xix, 445 pages. Hardbound. € 110.00. ISBN 3-598-24441-X

From medieval chorales, to light operetta, to electronically generated 'musique concrete', this title offers meticulous coverage of musical composition and criticism, past and present. Information Sources in Music is an easy-to-use, evaluative guide to the wide range of published sources of information available.

Arranged by subject, each entry includes a brief description of the source, frequency of publication, and price and serial information where appropriate. As a time-saving resource this title will enable researchers to go straight to the information they need, indicating the range of sources available and offering a means of assessing which are the most useful.

K · G · Saur Verlag
A Part of The Thomson Corporation

Postfach 70 16 20 · 81316 München · Germany
Tel. +49 (0)89 769 02-300 · Fax +49 (0)89 769 02-150/ 250
e-mail: saur.info@thomson.com   http://www.saur.de

K · G · Saur Verlag

Mary Trim

Growing and Knowing:
A selection guide for children's literature

2004. XXVI, 253 pages
Hardbound
€ 88.00
ISBN 3-598-11581-4

This is the essential reference work for professionals who work with children and their books. It will be used as a reference tool in children's libraries and resource centres, as well as in general reference libraries.

It provides a guide to the selection of books for children, recognising the vast range of books published and the individual rates of reading and social development of different children.

The book is divided into two sections. The first provides information on appropriate books for different reading levels and recommends titles of children's books. Each title is evaluated according to the latest research criteria in the field, with a full explanation of why it has been chosen. The second section provides invaluable advice for the librarian on the promotion of children's books.

The author, Mary Trim was until recently, a lecturer at Loughborough University, UK and has spent twenty-five years of her professional life lecturing in children's literature at universities in England and Australia.

www.saur.de

Alina Vickery, Brian Vickery

Information Science in Theory and Practice

2004. XIV, 400 pages
Hardbound
€ 110.00
ISBN 3-598-11658-6

This classic student and professional text has been a main stay of the information profession for many years and is regularly cited. It has been reprinted many times and now this newly revised 3rd edition covers some of the most recent changes to affect the profession.

The effect of the internet and its role in the area of information science and librarianship is examined thoroughly through the addition of a new chapter. The internet is also considered in relation to other topics within this book and relates to the issues arising from its use in the collection and dissemination of information.

A feature of this book is the "Map of Information Science", completely updated to reflect the profession as it is today. References have also been updated. This is an essential work for anyone working in the field of information science and librarianship and will contribute considerably to the literature of the profession.

Brian C. Vickery, Professor Emeritus, University College, London, is one of the foremost specialists in this area and his work is renowned internationally.

K·G·Saur Verlag
A Part of The Thomson Corporation

Postfach 70 16 20 · 81316 München · Germany
Tel. +49 (0)89 7 69 02-300 · Fax +49 (0)89 7 69 02-150/ 250
e-mail: saur.info@thomson.com http://www.saur.de

K·G·Saur Verlag

THOMSON

Kenneth A. Megill

Thinking for a Living:
The Coming Age of Knowledge Work

2004. XIV, 193 pages
Hardbound
€ 78.00
ISBN 3-598-11638-1

Knowledge Management as a term has been around for more than a decade, but do we really know what it means? This far-reaching book tackles the thorny question of how to define knowledge management and make it work in the 21st century.

It questions our beliefs in the role of the information profession and tells us how to become information workers of the future by providing advice on overcoming the challenges facing the library profession. It develops the idea of the knowledge culture and knowledge work and goes on to expand how information needs to be shared and not hoarded as in the traditional role of libraries as keepers of knowledge (From Cooperation to Collaboration, Integrated Digital Environment, Communities of Practice, Practice of Transformation). **Thinking for a Living** provides a clear and very accessible practical framework for knowledge work.

This excellent book provides an insight into the future of the information profession and outlines the skills necessary for the knowledge worker of the future. It is essential for all information professionals and will prove to be a classic work.

Dr. Kenneth A. Megill is a consultant and writer with extensive experience of the information world.

www.saur.de

K·G·Saur Verlag
A Part of The Thomson Corporation

Postfach 70 16 20 · 81316 München · Germany
Tel. +49 (0)89 7 69 02-300 · Fax +49 (0)89 7 69 02-150/ 250
e-mail: saur.info@thomson.com   http://www.saur.de